By The Grace of God

or

It Ain't All Luck

By

Al Zlaten

By The Grace of God

First Printing 2000

Al Zlaten, Publisher
1673 Brown Ct
Longmont, Colorado
80503

ISBN 0-9676796-0-5

Printed in the USA by:
Morris Publishing
3212 East Highway 30
Kearney, NE
68847
1-800-650-7888

Front Cover
The author just before take-off on a combat mission from an airstrip near Jodoigne, Belgium (1945).

Dedication

This book is written in recognition and thanksgiving for Divine intervention without which it would have been highly unlikely that I would have survived the situations in which I found myself during World War II.

To Bruce Stafford

Al [illegible]

Acknowledgments

The contents of this book were basically completed several years ago, while my memory of my experiences in WWII were still very vivid. Over the years my wife, LaVon, continued to encourage me to work on the book to get it into final form.

Thanks to my daughter, Vivian, for typing and retyping the manuscript during many corrections and revisions. Thanks to my grandson Matt for using his computer skills to properly format the manuscript for printing. Also thanks to the family members and friends who encouraged me to put my story into print.

Prologue

It was to be my 36th mission. It started with a three hour delay as we waited, in our P-47 fighter planes, for the weather to clear over enemy lines. Finally we were cleared for takeoff and I took my place as leader of the second element in the lead flight.

Our squadron of twelve planes crossed over enemy lines to the usual greeting of enemy antiaircraft fire. The front was overcast and the ground was visible only through occasional breaks in the clouds. After flying several minutes into enemy territory, I sighted a truck convoy traveling through the mountains west of the Rhine River. I reported my sighting to the squadron leader who had not seen the convoy. He ordered me to lead the dive bombing attack on the truck convoy below. I called my wingman to follow me down. Clouds were obscuring the ground but I could see the convoy through openings in the clouds and completed my bomb run.

As I pulled off the target, I saw forty millimeter antiaircraft tracers and suddenly my plane was hit. Engine oil covered the windshield and flames whipped past the left side of the cockpit! In just a few seconds, the engine stopped completely and I began to lose altitude. I knew I was in trouble.

INTRODUCTION

For information for my family, friends and readers and to illustrate that good things "happen" to ordinary people, biographical information is included at the beginning of this book.

I was born August 13, 1921 near the Puritan Coal Camp in a small community called White House, located several miles east of the Rocky Mountains in Colorado. The name White House came from a boarding house (painted white) that was torn down after the nearby coal mine was mined out and closed. My father was a coal miner and my two brothers, Joe and Fred, joined him in the mines not long after getting through the first eight grades of school. I was the youngest, and while they were becoming coal miners I was just beginning grade school.

There were nearly a dozen children in our community, some older and some near my age. Our playground in the White House community was the open space across the road, and to the rear of our homes. Across the road was an abandoned mine shaft that had been partially backfilled so the shaft was only about twenty feet deep. With the help of the older boys we excavated a sloping ledge into the shaft so we could get in and out of the shaft. The nearly filled shaft wasn't considered a very hazardous play area. In the rear of the last house, in the row of houses along the road, there was an area where coal slack had been spread in layers after a formerly existing coal mine had been abandoned. By spontaneous combustion, the coal slack had become ignited and burned continuously over a wide area. On a cold, wet day wisps of smoke covered the area and the smell of burning coal filled the air. There was a narrow path, through this field of burning coal slack, which led to an abandoned coal mine shaft that was more than a hundred feet deep. A single strand of barbed wire, attached to four unsteady posts, marked the location of the shaft. This was not one of our approved play areas. The narrow path through the burning coal slack was like a maze through a series of hazards. My cousin Fred, about my age, stepped off the path into the burning slack and was severely burned and has scarred ankles as a reminder of our days at White House.

I'm sure our guardian angels worked overtime to keep us from being injured. One experience returns to mind. A neighbor owned a Model "T" with a front seat and an open box in the rear. The driver sat on the seat and the passengers rode in back in the box. Usually we stood up in the box. I had not started school yet, so I must have been about five years old at the time of the incident. While traveling down a dirt road, the front wheels of the Model "T" would suddenly jerk uncontrollably from side to side. True to form, the wheels jerked from side to side and I was tossed out of the box and made a five-point landing (forehead, elbows and knees) on the graveled road. Aside from being frightened I suffered no broken bones, just holes in my clothing at the elbows and knees and a scratched forehead. I climbed back into the truck box and we drove on home, only this time I sat down in the truck box. My friend Ed, the driver, who was my older brother's age, gave me a dime so I wouldn't tell my mom I had fallen out of the truck while it was moving. My torn clothing and scratched forehead was to be explained by saying I tripped and fell while running. On seeing me, my mother immediately asked what had happened to me. I told her I had fallen while running, but being a mother, she knew better and finally I blurted out the truth. She was visibly disturbed but thankful I wasn't seriously injured. Mark one up for my guardian angel.

Life was difficult for all the families who depended on employment in the coal mines. The mines worked steadily during the fall, winter and spring months when the demand for coal remained constant. However, in the summer, most miners worked about one day a week or less. It was necessary for families to save for the lean summer months, since there was no such thing as unemployment compensation or welfare in those days.

During my first four grades in school I rode the bus, together with other children from the mining community. We were bussed to the small town of Erie, Colorado, which to this day remains a small community and is just now beginning to experience growth that had been in progress for several years in other towns and cities in Colorado.

When I was eleven years old, my father bought a small farm in Boulder County about eight miles west of the coal camp and closer to the Rocky Mountains. He constructed a small frame house on the land and my mother and I joined him on the farm. My two brothers remained in the house that we owned and continued to work in the mines. My next five years of schooling (grades five through nine) were in the Canfield School, located in the small settlement of Canfield, Colorado, with a population of less than one hundred. The school was about two miles from our farm, if you walked along the railroad track which passed within a short distance of the school yard. Walking was the normal method of getting to and from school. On the few winter days when the temperature was way below zero, one of my parents would take me to school in our Model T Ford. I didn't have to walk to school alone, as I was joined by other students who lived nearby. As I recall, there were only two rooms for the nine grades in the school. The multigrade school rooms were not the best for learning purposes. The Canfield School building was torn down many years ago and the land used for housing construction.

During the summer I was fully occupied helping with all types of farm work. Part of our farm was used for vegetable farming which proved to be very labor intensive, and I was busy from dawn till dusk. In the winter I found time to go hunting small game that was abundant along the creek not too far from our house.

After completing the ninth grade, to continue my education , I went to the high school at Erie, Colorado, where I had gone the first four years of grade school. Going back to school in Erie provided the opportunity to become re-acquainted with some of my childhood friends I had known earlier.

Because Erie High School was about four miles from our farmhouse, walking to school was not considered to be practical. For one thing, walking to school would be too time consuming and I needed to get home from school as quickly as possible to help with the chores on the farm. So the decision was made; I would drive the family car to school. I thought it was a good idea. Our Model T Ford had been replaced with a 1932 Ford Coupe which I drove to high school for three years. I had been driving the Model T for several years and graduating to the 1932 Ford Coupe was a real treat. Since driver's licenses were not required, age was not a problem. Practically all of the students in high school lived in Erie or came to school by bus. Less than a half dozen of the students were privileged enough to drive to school. Those of us who had a car at high school were the envy of the other students. Today the situation is vastly different as the high school parking lots are overflowing with students who drive to school. While at Erie High I participated in sports as long as the sports schedule did not interfere with required work on the farm. I graduated in the top half of the class and was prepared to go to college. My parents never intended that I should work in the coal mines as my older brothers did.

CHAPTER ONE

The University of Colorado and Civilian Pilot Training

In the fall of 1939, I and several of my classmates from Erie High and friends from the neighboring town of Lafayette, Colorado were planning on attending the University of Colorado at Boulder. None of us could afford to live on campus in the dormitory or in nearby apartments; consequently, as a matter of necessity, we lived at home and commuted daily to classes. Obviously we did not fit into the upper caste social system, but there were many students on campus who accepted our friendship even though we lived way off campus. My first year was a shock academically. High school did not prepare one for the rigors of college studies.

During my first year, I played on the freshman football squad as linebacker. I don't know if we ever had a freshman team, since we played no scheduled games. However, we played a lot of football against the varsity team. Actually, we were termed "cannon fodder" for the varsity. We scrimmaged the varsity every day. I played mostly on defense and if at anytime a freshman player made a good play and made a varsity player look bad, there was instant retaliation by the varsity team on the next play. The overzealous "frosh" player was double-teamed and soundly smashed. At one hundred fifty-five pounds I was too light to play linebacker, and as a result was battered and bruised after each scrimmage. My colleague at the other linebacker position who was not one pound heavier than I , also suffered from the physical contact. One afternoon, during the scrimmage with the varsity, we were both having a bruising time tackling the varsity's all conference fullback who ran over and through the freshman defensive line. My colleague became a brother at arms when we both agreed that we had taken enough punishment from the varsity fullback, whom we had to tackle on nearly every play. We decided that the next time the big fullback came through the porous freshman line, we would both tackle him. One of us would hit him high and the other hit him low. It wasn't long before we got our chance and with calculated determination we both tackled the big fullback. There was a bone jarring collision and we both picked ourselves up slowly. We looked at the fullback who was being helped as he limped off the field. My linebacker colleague and I nodded at each other as if to say "Well, we won't have to tackle him anymore today". The freshman coach looked at us and we detected a slight smile on his usually stern face. The varsity coach was unhappy with the result of our defensive play and expressed his disapproval to the freshman coach, who shrugged his shoulders and dismissed the incident as part of football. As I recall, jarring the varsity fullback was probably the highlight of my college football experience.

My sophomore year's studies left no time for sports. However, the spring of my sophomore year, (1941) provided an extra curricular activity that would have a major influence in my life. The war in Europe had been going on for nearly two years and many of the top government officials, including President F. D. Roosevelt, knew and perhaps secretly hoped the United States would be "forced" to declare war on the Axis nations. As part of the preparation for war, the Federal Government started a Civilian Pilot Training (CPT) program at a number of colleges and universities throughout the country. The University of Colorado at Boulder was one of the universities selected for this program. I was eager to find out how I could participate in such a program and learn to fly. I had been interested in airplanes and flying since my pre-teen years when I built balsa wood model airplanes and read stories of the World War I battle aces. However, I could never realistically believe I would be able to take flying lessons since the cost of flying instruction was beyond my financial means. Actually, my parents were giving all they had to help pay for the expenses of my going to the University. To put it in today's politically correct language, we were financially challenged. Qualifications to be selected for the CPT program were established and those included passing a physical examination, which cost ten dollars, and written permission from both parents to participate in the CPT program. Passing the physical examination was no problem, but persuading both my mother and father to grant permission to take flying lessons was not easy. Both of my parents were convinced that flying was dangerous and people who risked their lives flying had to be less than sane. I knew that obtaining my parents' written consent to partake in an activity they both believed to be dangerous would be difficult. Neither my mother nor my father relished the idea of being individually responsible for permitting me to take flying training. My only hope was to convince my mother that my father thought it (taking CPT) was all right and to convince my father that it was OK with my mother. So, I told my mother that "Dad would sign the consent form if you would", and I told my father that mom said she "would sign if you would". I wouldn't want to vouch for the truthfulness of my statement to my mother and father; however, after several days of my pleading, both my parents signed the consent form permitting me to take CPT training.

CPT trainees were required to take several hours of ground school classes along with the flight training. Ground school classes were held in the evening. Consequently, I didn't get home from the University until 10:30 at night.

Fortunately, the ground school was completed in the Spring before flying lessons began in June of 1941.

A Cub J-3 aircraft with a 65 horse powered engine was the aircraft used during this primary stage of flight training. The Spring semester at the University was over, but flying lessons continued throughout the Summer. My flying lessons were scheduled for 4:00 p.m. or later which gave me time to put in a full day's work on the farm. Sometimes flying lessons were scheduled every other day and sometimes lessons were scheduled every day. I made it a point to be punctual so as not to irritate my flying instructor, because I truly wanted to pass the course and go on to the next stage of flight training. Primary flight training was completed with only one memorable incident. During a solo cross country flight, I had to fly to Denver, Ft. Collins and return to Boulder. The first leg of the flight was to Denver. As I approached the Denver area, visibility became poor and I flew into a local fog bank. I was unprepared for the loss of the visible horizon; however, I started to make a slow 180 degree turn to fly back out of the fog bank. (At this stage of flight training I had no instrument flying training.) I continued to make a gentle turn and flew out of the fog bank where the natural horizon was a welcome sight. I had a narrow escape from a dangerous situation, and as time went on I learned how potentially dangerous it is flying into a fog bank without instrument flight training.

Primary CPT training was successfully completed and the next step would be secondary CPT flight training. In less than one month (28 days) secondary flight training began! In secondary we were going to fly the Waco UPF-7 biplane. The UPF-7 had a 220 horsepower engine and was approved for aerobatics. CPT flying training was beginning to be fun! I was flying an open cockpit biplane and wearing a helmet and goggles just like the pilots of WW I and the barnstormers after the war.

Flying the Waco UPF-7 was a great experience for a lad off the farm. I concentrated on learning to do the required aerobatic maneuvers and flying the UPF-7 was almost becoming second nature and I felt comfortable in the open cockpit biplane. On one of my scheduled flying days I decided to practice my aerobatics over our farm so my mom and dad could watch. I flew the plane through various loops and rolls that would show how well I could fly. When I returned home later that afternoon I asked my mom and dad how they enjoyed the aerobatics. They both asked me what was wrong with the plane. They both commented that the plane didn't fly very straight and they were concerned that something was wrong. Evidently they both thought that if an airplane is not flying straight and level, something is wrong. They said they were relieved when I flew by straight and level and waved to them. Thereafter I made it a point to fly straight and level when I flew over our farm.

One Saturday morning I was scheduled for a solo flight, so the day before I told a group of young boys in Erie, Colorado that I would be west of the school, at a certain time, doing aerial acrobatics. That Saturday morning I flew over the school and waved at the dozen or so boys sitting on the curb. For the next fifteen or twenty minutes I performed all of the aerobatic maneuvers I had learned, being careful to keep my flying far enough to the west so I was not flying over any populated areas. I didn't particularly relish the thought of being reported for violating flying regulations. That evening I drove to Erie where I encountered some of the youngsters I had entertained with my aerobatics and, judging from their comments, I was sure they were impressed by the farm boy turned aviator.

Carl, one of my close friends, lived with his widowed mother, sisters and brother, near the coal mining community where I lived as a young boy. I had promised him I would "buzz" their house some Saturday morning. On the following Saturday, I pointed the UPF-7 toward the coal mining community that consisted of five remaining houses. Within fifteen minutes I sighted my friend Carl's house. I put the airplane in a dive and flew over the house at treetop level. The occupants of the house, my friend's mother, Annie, his sisters Frances and Joanie and brother, Al,. all came rushing out. Carl, who had just driven out of the driveway, stopped and watched from his car. I banked the biplane around and made a low fly-by, waved to my friends below and headed back toward my home airport. That evening I drove to Carl's home, as was my custom on Saturday nights, for we were good friends since childhood and palled around on Saturday nights. Carl's mother scolded me for rattling the dishes in her cupboard by my buzz job. Those were fun days.

However, on December 7, 1941 with the Japanese attack on Pearl Harbor, life became significantly more somber. The fact that we were at war with Japan did not come as a total surprise. I had diligently studied numerous articles and news reports from the Orient and it was clear that our attitude toward Japan's war of expansion was becoming more threatening. I had predicted that we would be at war with Japan by January, 1942. Yes, I missed by one month. Surely, if I , an average college student could see the coming world events, our leaders in Washington should have known that the threat of war with Japan was imminent, but that's another story and I deviate from my primary intent in this writing.

Along with the change in tone of everyday life, my CPT flying training was approached with a more serious attitude. Aerobatics were still fun and I managed to unintentionally do some stunts the biplane was not designed to do. One day while doing solo aerobatics I stalled the aircraft going straight up and the plane began falling tail first. I moved the controls rapidly but they were ineffective. I had visions of having to use the parachute that was a standard requirement for all who flew in CPT. I took a quick glance at the tail section to see if the tail was still in one piece; it was. Then I applied full power and full left rudder and left aileron and eased into a normal spin and recovered quickly. For certain maneuvers each type of aerobatically stressed aircraft has a minimum required airspeed necessary to successfully complete the maneuver. This lesson is usually re-learned for each type of aircraft flown.

Secondary CPT was successfully completed and the next phase was Cross Country Training which would lead to a Flight Instructor's Rating. I was accepted for this phase of training which began in the Summer of 1942. A group of five of us trainees from around the state of Colorado began the training. We stayed in the Sigma Chi house on the Colorado State University campus in Ft. Collins, Colorado. Here we flew a Waco cabin plane from the Ft. Collins airport. Everything went well during the first few weeks of training, then things took a turn for the worse for me. I became ill with a protracted case of influenza and didn't fly for several days. I was worried about falling behind in the accelerated training schedule and chose to try to fly while still suffering with influenza. It didn't work out, I became ill during several flights and could not proceed with my training. The instructors decided I was falling too far behind and would have to drop the course. My plans for getting a Flight Instructor's Rating were suddenly smashed.

After a couple of weeks I felt I was recovered from the influenza, but it was too late to continue in the CPT program. I notified my Draft Board I was no longer in the CPT program and was immediately classified 1A.

Prior to the call to duty with fiancee LaVon Brown.

A mantel full of morale boosters.

CHAPTER TWO
Call To Military Service

Young men were being drafted into the armed forces every week and I had no desire to be drafted into the infantry. I knew in my heart that I could fly. On August 3, 1942 my good friend Frank and I went to Denver to enlist in the Army Air Corps. We both passed the physical and were accepted in the Air Corps. We were told to go home and await orders. When we received written orders, Frank was instructed to await further orders and I was instructed to go back to the University of Colorado and attend classes until further notice. Several of my friends at the University had enlisted in the Air Corps and were also instructed to continue schooling until further notice. In the fall of 1942 I started my senior year at the University of Colorado. During this time I missed the flying I had been doing the past two years.

On January 23, 1943 all Air Corps Reservists attending the University were ordered to report for active duty. The long expected call had finally arrived. On February 23, 1943 I took Frank to Denver and saw him off to active duty in the Army Air Corps. Five days later my friend Carl took me to Denver where I reported to Union Station (railroad station). Along with many other young men, I boarded a train which took us to Jefferson Barracks, Missouri for basic training. Basic training, it is said by some, will make a man of you or kill you. I'm not convinced it makes you more of a man, but I do know that several young men died of pneumonia or spinal meningitis at Jefferson Barracks. The available hospital facilities were so inadequate that the hallways were full of army cots provided for the continuous stream of sick inductees. The major objective of most of the trainees was to stay out of the hospital and to keep warm in the bitter cold weather. Army tents pitched over a wood floor were the sleeping quarters for newly inducted young men. Each tent was provided with a pot-bellied coal stove for heat. Unless the stove was re-supplied with coal during the night, there would be no heat in the tent by early morning. Basic training at Jefferson Barracks was a memorable, though a very unpleasant, experience. For most of us inductees at Jefferson Barracks, it was the first time we were away from home for any extended period. Nearly everyone was homesick and together with the miserable weather and physically exhausting basic training, there was little to be happy about. It was one of those times you felt like crying, but resisted the feeling. Yet everyone perked up and smiles began to emerge as "mail call" produced letters from home. Indeed it was the letters from home, especially from the sweetheart that was left behind, that boosted morale and gave one the strength to make it through the misery of basic training. The letters from LaVon boosted my morale more than anything. The thought that there was a special girl at home, whose never ending letters spoke of never ending love, was most comforting during a most uncomfortable period of my life.

After a month of basic training the day came when we were to leave Jefferson Barracks for our next destination. I was overjoyed, but my joy was short lived when at the train station I discovered that departees were being given a physical examination and those who were sick were being detained. I had been running a high fever for several days and did not report to sick bay lest I be put in the hospital. I knew that if one of the doctors looked at me I'd be detained at Jefferson Barracks. I saw the line of men being given a brief physical exam and I observed the line of men coming out buttoning their shirts and buckling their belts. I saw a friend buttoning his shirt and asked him if they were checking names on the roll and he said “no”. I stepped in behind him and acted as though I was buttoning my shirt and buckling my belt, and so I successfully detoured the doctor’s examination line and avoided the chance of being detained. Mark one up for quick thinking. We left Jefferson Barracks at 1:50 a.m. on March 24, 1943 and arrived in St. Paul, Minnesota at 12:30 a.m. the next day. We were assigned rooms in the dormitories of McAlester College in St. Paul and got to sleep at 4:00 a.m. I still carried a fever and on the second day I was taken to the Fort Snelling Army Hospital in Minneapolis. The hospital at Fort Snelling was a big improvement compared to the overcrowded, poorly staffed hospital at Jefferson Barracks. Within three days I was well again and back to McAlester College. I later found out that conditions at Jefferson Barracks were so bad that noted news commentator Walter Winchell called for a congressional investigation of the Army training facility. I understand his efforts improved conditions. I clearly remember saying to myself “If I can live through Jefferson Barracks, I’ll live through the war”.

McAlester College was a small school with a compact campus which included dormitories, the majority of which we occupied. Now that we were through with basic training we were called Aviation Students. That was fair enough since we were at a college and were going to take various courses for six weeks. The new rank of Aviation Student carried the same old Buck Private’s pay of one dollar per day. I can remember writing home for money so I could have a studio photograph taken to send home.

All the aviation related subjects that were taught in our classes were familiar to me, as I had taken the courses in CPT training. One course we took was a shocker to most of the Aviation Students at McAlester. For some unknown reason everyone had to take the college physics course during our stay at McAlester. I had just finished a college physics course at Colorado University prior to induction into the military. This gave me an unfair advantage over the other students, most of whom had little or no schooling beyond high school. Before I left McAlester College for the Western Training Command, the young instructor of the physics course informed me I was the only one in the class that passed the course. Passing the accelerated college course was obviously not a requirement for continuing our Air Corps training.

Our stay at McAlester College was to be for approximately three months; however, without notice (the military never was much for giving personnel advanced notice), a small group of us were ordered to prepare to move to Santa Ana, California for Cadet Training. We left the next day, May 22, 1943, by train.

Santa Ana Cadet Training Base

We were all looking forward to being Aviation Cadets, but much to our chagrin we were told we would train as Aviation Students for six weeks to see how many of us could qualify to become Aviation Cadets. The training consisted of marching and physical training (PT) with some elementary courses on weather and navigation. Qualifying for Cadets proved to be a matter of passing a physical examination which eliminated a small number of students, primarily for failing the eye exam. The students who failed were re-assigned to training as ground crew or bomber air crew or whatever the need was. The rest of us continued to march and take PT and more PT until one day we were pronounced ready to be Aviation Cadets.

Being promoted from Aviation Student to Aviation Cadet had several benefits. GI blouses (coats) were exchanged for Cadet blouses, the pay was increased to seventy five dollars per month and the food was better than what we were used to as Aviation Students. The reason for the better food became evident on the end of the month pay voucher, where we were informed that ten dollars was deducted from our pay for the better food. We were assured that all cadets were in favor of the deduction. So much for the improvements; we still marched everyday and had PT and more PT with the usual classroom work on elementary weather, navigation and basic theory of flight. However, the nemesis of our studies was a class in sending and receiving Morse code. Most of us struggled to pass this never-used system of communication. Six weeks of Aviation Cadet training in Class 44-C and we were getting ready to go to Primary Flying Training! As usual, everyone was given a physical examination prior to shipping out. Everyone's name was being checked off, but this was no big deal, so I thought. During the physical exam it was detected that I had a slight fever. I was told to check in at the hospital to be sure - still no big deal.

CHAPTER THREE

Six More Weeks Of Aviation Cadet Training

At the hospital I was examined and found to have two degrees of fever. No one seemed to know what was wrong, so I was put into the quarantined ward for a week. In the meantime my classmates in 44-C shipped out to their various assigned primary flying training bases.

As a result of my confinement for a slight fever of undetermined cause I was held over and assigned to Aviation Cadet Class 44-D for six more weeks of the same training I had just completed. I've never quite figured out why I was held over; perhaps there was a reason.

Friends that I had made in Class 44-C were gone and new friendships needed to be established. One pleasant surprise was finding several fellows, whom I left at McAlester College in St. Paul, were in Class 44-D. Since I had completed six weeks of Aviation Cadet training as a member of Class 44-C, I was looked upon as an old hand. I passed on tips on what was required during weekly inspections to avoid receiving demerits. Demerits could lead to loss of weekend passes and result in mandatory hours of solo marching around the barracks at the rate of one hour for every demerit over seven. It was not unusual to see several cadets marching off demerits with rifles on their shoulders. I learned early that marching off demerits was something to avoid and, although it was virtually impossible to avoid demerits, I never exceeded the allowable number of seven in one week. In some instances demerits were issued without rhyme or reason. As an example, I received demerits for having dust on my second pair of shoes during an inspection on the Saturday I was in the hospital. Logical? Maybe it was to some of the "bird-brains" that conducted the inspection.

A second six weeks of cadet training came to a close and Class 44-D was split up and assigned to several different primary flight training schools.

Primary Flight Training At Tulare, California

Duties at primary flight training were more enjoyable than training at Santa Ana. Although marching was still a part of activities, it was reduced to a tolerable minimum. Flight students had to cope with a new stress that accompanied learning how to fly the open cockpit Stearman biplanes used at the Tex Rankin Flight School at Tulare, California. No one ever asked if any of us had ever flown an airplane before. No one asked and I never volunteered any information. As a cadet you learned to say "Yes sir, no sir and no excuse, sir" and that's all.

While most of the cadets were having the normal difficulties learning to fly the Stearman biplane, I found myself very comfortable flying the plane. The Stearman was not much different from the Waco UPF-7 I had flown in CPT training. I did so well that my instructor allowed me to fly solo after only six hours of dual training. I was the first to "solo" among the several hundred cadets and after landing and parking the plane, I was dunked in a barrel of water as part of a ritual that happened to the first cadet to solo. The next day the Commanding Officer of the flying school issued an order stating that no cadet was to solo with less than ten hours of dual flight time. After several more hours of flying with my instructor he began to realize that I was progressing more rapidly than any of his previous or present students. His inevitable question brought out my admission that I had previously flown in CPT. This knowledge eventually got to the Civilian Commander of the flight school and he decided to give me a check ride. I wasn't particularly nervous with the thought since I knew I could fly. Little did I realize that the Civilian Commander didn't care for CPT trainees. I also didn't realize that I was being "set-up". The day for the check ride arrived and before we climbed into the plane, the Civilian Commander said, "If you over rev the engine on any maneuver I'm going to fail you on the ride". I nodded and figured that would be no problem. I climbed into the rear cockpit, looked at the instrument panel and saw a hole where one of the instruments was missing. The tachometer had been removed from the rear cockpit! We took off and I flew through all of the maneuvers requested and was careful not to over rev the engine. We landed, got out of the plane, and he informed me that was the worst ride he ever had; and I under-revved every maneuver and he was failing me on the ride. I had a few thoughts go through my mind but I didn't say anything; cadets were not supposed to say anything but "Yes sir, no sir and no excuse, sir". When I told my instructor what happened, he was more than a little upset. I didn't know it at the time, but he considered me to be his best student. He said he would get me another check ride the next day with another instructor pilot. The next day I passed the check ride with flying colors. From that time on, primary flight training was a breeze; I received only the minimum required dual time with my instructor, since he told me he needed to spend more time with his other four students. I was told to go and practice any maneuvers that I thought I needed to polish up.

Everyday that I flew solo in the Stearman I enjoyed doing all sorts of aerobatics, but I most of all enjoyed doing the inverted falling leaf maneuver I had learned in CPT. During one maneuver I managed to get into an inverted flat spin. In the early days of flying, it was difficult and on some occasions impossible to recover from an inverted flat spin. I had never been in an inverted flat spin, but somehow I maneuvered the plane from the inverted flat spin into a normal spin and recovered control of the Stearman. I always made sure I had plenty of altitude when practicing aerobatics. I even got used to the engine quitting during inverted flight. Since the radial engines in the Stearman were not fuel injected, the engines would quit when the plane was flown upside down for any length of time, but they always started up again when the plane was turned right side up.

Several of my cadet friends became aware of the freedom I had been given by my instructor to fly solo everyday and asked me what I did during my solo flying. "Lots of aerobatics and I buzz a few swimming pools among the orange groves in the countryside", was my reply. Buzzing swimming pools intrigued some of the cadets, and the next thing I knew a couple of cadets were called on the carpet for buzzing nearby swimming pools. The residents at the buzzed swimming pools were a bit annoyed and had called the Commanding Officer at the flying school and reported the identification numbers of the plane doing the buzzing. A few days later I had a chance to talk with the cadet pilots who were reprimanded for buzzing. The cadets asked me if I still buzzed swimming pools, "Yes," I replied, "but not everyday". "How do you keep from getting caught?" they asked. "First, let me guess how you both buzzed the pools. You buzzed the pool then you made a big, slow turn to look at the pool you buzzed, right?" They both nodded. "You dipped the wings making a slow turn and the people on the ground had an easy view of the big ID number on your plane." I continued, "When I buzz one of the pools located next to a house in the orange grove, I come in real low with lots of speed from a dive and stay low and fly straight away from the residence. That way I don't stick around very long and the ID number on the plane is almost impossible to see."

Graduation day at Primary Flight Training School was drawing near and no one wanted to get washed out, so all flight rules were followed by all; but it (buzzing) was fun while it lasted. Practically all of the cadets graduated and were passed on to Basic Flight Training. Tragically, during primary training, we lost one cadet who was caught in a fast developing fog and was fatally injured when he crashed.

CHAPTER FOUR

Basic, Advanced And Transitional Flight Training

Basic flight training was next. We traveled to Gardner Field at Taft, California where we were housed in barracks right next to the runways. BT-13 Vultee low wing airplanes were used for flight training. To some of us, the BT-13, which we called the Vultee Vibrator, was an under powered, noisy airplane. At Gardner Field we were introduced to formation flying and night flying, which I enjoyed. I did miss the aerobatics that I used to do in the Stearman biplane, but serious aerobatics in the BT-13 were not part of our curriculum in basic flight training. My stay at Gardner Field was not very eventful and the course was completed without any significant occurrences.

Next was Advanced Training and we all looked forward to flying the North American AT-6 (Advanced Trainer) which had more power and was a lot more maneuverable than the cumbersome Vultee Vibrator. For advanced training we were moved to Luke Field near Phoenix, Arizona. Luke Field, situated in a desert area, was known for good flying weather. The area was surrounded by mountains which were formidable but not as high and spectacular as the mountains near Boulder, Colorado, where I took my CPT flight training. Advanced Flight Training was more intense than Basic Flight Training. We were introduced to instrument flying, in the aircraft and in the primitive Link trainer. In addition to instrument flying we were introduced to and began training in aerial gunnery, ground gunnery and dive bombing. The days were long and busy, but flying the AT-6 was enjoyable. Formation flying in the AT-6 was easier than in the BT-13, due not only to a better aircraft, but also to more proficient cadet flying mates. With all of the gunnery training, instrument flying, dive bombing, and long solo cross country flights, we began to understand that we were training for eventual combat. The training was more intense and more risky as attested by the increase in fatal accidents. A total of six cadets and two instructors were killed in the three month period at Luke Field.

One of the requirements of advanced training was to fly the Curtis P-40 fighter aircraft made famous by the Flying Tigers in China. However, the P-40's at Luke Field were not painted with the bared-tooth nose of the Flying Tigers. Since there was only a single seat in the P-40 there was no instructor to go with you on your first solo flight. Preparation consisted of reading the P-40 Flight Manual, lectures by instructors and one hour of sitting in the cockpit and memorizing the positioning of all switches, controls and instruments. After all of the preparation, the memorable day came and you made your first flight in a real fighter plane! The roar of the big engine and the excessive rudder pressure needed to keep the plane straight during takeoff was enough to keep your attention at peak level. Ten hours of flying in the P-40 finished our training at Luke Field and we graduated, received our wings and were commissioned as 2nd Lieutenants in the Army Air Corps.

We were all on orders to proceed to our next assignment. The complete order was read and a long list of names of those going to Baton Rouge, Louisiana for processing was monotonously read off. As the officer reading the names neared the end, alphabetically, he stated that the following officers will report to the Pacific Theater of Operations. I thought to myself, "O, nuts, I'm going to the Pacific!" The officer read off the names until he came to the last name on the list, (which was mine,) and "Alexander Zlaten will proceed to Harding Field, Baton Rouge, Louisiana". What a relief; I would go to Europe with my friends. What happened with the orders? Someone called for twenty-seven pilots to go to the Pacific, and whoever counted the last twenty-seven on the list miscounted, and I was the twenty-eighth and last one on the list. That was too close for comfort. I did not particularly care to fly missions in the Pacific area, where most of the flying would be over water.

Before reporting to Harding Field in Baton Rouge, Louisiana, all of the newly graduated cadets - now Lieutenants - were given a delay on route (home leave) of almost two weeks. This was the first home leave in fourteen months and was certainly looked forward to with great anticipation! Reunion with my mother and father was certainly enjoyable. However, reunion with my steady girl, LaVon Brown, was a long looked forward to event. LaVon worked every day, so most of my days were spent at home and all of the evenings were spent with her. While on leave I received orders cutting my leave time short and ordering me to report to Harding Field a couple of days early. As was evidenced on my arrival at Harding Field, no one there asked for our early arrival and our schedule was not accelerated one bit. It was just the military way to indicate that you were still under someone else's control. Anyway, I had sufficient time at home to become engaged to LaVon before I left for Baton Rouge, Louisiana. Parting a second time from family and my sweetheart, now my fiancé, was saddening and the thought of going to war was ever in the background.

Harding Field

A large number of newly commissioned pilots were on the train going to Harding Field and I had met many of them at advanced training at Luke Field.

Baton Rouge, Louisiana was hot and humid in late April of 1944. At Harding Field, Fighter Pilot indoctrination was strictly ground school (classroom) classes. Emphasis was placed on flying safety, since combat flying has its own undeniable risks, bone-headed mistakes by pilots were avoidable and to this end the classes were worthwhile. My strongest memory of Harding Field was the hot, humid weather. One could put on a clean, pressed uniform and in less than an hour the uniform looked as though you had slept in it. I was also intrigued by the sight of the mighty Mississippi River, perched above the city, and contained by the levee. There were P-47's flying at the field but we only heard them and saw them in the air. There was no flying for us during our three week stay . So much for Harding Field this trip.

Bruning, Nebraska P-47 Transition Training

When we boarded the train to leave Baton Rouge, all we knew for sure was that we were going to Nebraska for P-47 flight training. Our destination turned out to be Bruning, Nebraska. This information was leaked out to us after nearly 24 hours of traveling aboard the troop train. Bruning, Nebraska was a small country settlement of less than a half dozen dwellings in farm country. Since the railroad did not pass through Bruning, we were bussed from the nearest railroad siding to the airfield that was to be our training base for the next three months.

Bruning Field consisted of an asphalt surfaced runway, a hangar for aircraft maintenance, one-story wooden huts (to house P-47 pilot trainees), an officer's club, mess hall and a gymnasium. Next to the hangar was a fire station housing the customary firemen and fire truck. There was nothing showy or luxurious about this military base, just the bare essentials. However, there was very little complaining from the newly commissioned fighter pilots; at least not at first. Much to our chagrin we discovered that the Commanding Officer was an old infantry Colonel. The Colonel made two errors in judgment; first he issued an order that all pilots would march to the flight line in formation. That raised a sour note among all of the newly commissioned pilots who had just completed fourteen months of cadet training where marching was an ever present, though not relished, part of our lives. As ordered, we "marched" to the flight line, out of step, in ragged formation of columns of twos, threes and sometimes unintentionally four abreast. The flight instructors assigned to duty at Bruning Field made a feeble attempt to get us to march in something resembling a military formation, but gave up quickly when we, as a group, announced that we had fulfilled our marching requirements and the Colonel's order was "for the birds". We were informed that we would be confined to base with no weekend passes. Big deal, we replied, there was nowhere to go on weekends, and most of us spent our weekends in the Officer's Club. The Colonel's marching order soon died a natural death.

Checking out and making our first flights in the P-47 fighter plane was a momentous occasion. While sitting in the roomy cockpit of the plane I memorized the location of all controls and instruments. Then came the test, while blindfolded I reached and touched each control and instrument in the order called out by the instructor. The cockpit test was passed and then came the first flight in the big 2000 horse powered fighter plane! The P-47 was more powerful, larger, heavier and faster than any of the planes I had flown to this time, both in the Air Corps and as a civilian. The first flight lasted less than an hour as I familiarized myself with the plane's reaction to control movement, throttle movement and stall characteristics. Let's be real, how familiar can you become with an airplane in less than an hour? Landing an airplane came naturally to me and I had no problems with my first landing in the P-47. Contrary to some statements of other P-47 pilots, I did not bond to the airplane and the airplane and I didn't become one, in fact, I didn't like the P-47. I originally would have preferred flying the P-51. After about ten hours of flying time in the P-47 I wasn't sure whether I was flying the plane or it was flying me. I mentioned this to one of the instructors and he suggested he fly along, in another P-47, and we would perform some high speed maneuvers and aerobatics. After an hour of high speed maneuvers I began to feel more comfortable flying the P-47, but, at the time, I still would have chosen to fly the P-51. I gave up that hope and resigned myself to perfecting my flying skills in the P-47, which after all, was a fighter plane. I did not elaborate extensively on many specific occurrences during my cadet training. However, I ask your indulgence as I recall a few more incidents during my P-47 transition training. Incidents I still remember clearly, therefore I assume they were significant.

Less than two weeks after arriving at Bruning Field we were informed that the invasion of Europe had begun, it was D-Day, June 6, 1944. I remember skipping lunch and going to a prayer service at noon. My main emotion was concern for the invasion troops and I felt fortunate that I was not one of the troops in the landing force. There was always the hope that the invasion forces would make rapid progress and make short work of the enemy.

After about two weeks of flying at Bruning Air Base, the infantry Colonel in command of the air base made his second error in judgment. Since his orders to have all pilots march to the flight line did not go over too well, he decided that all pilots would participate daily in two hours of directed PT (physical training). As cadets we exercised every day, rain or shine, and we had a belly full of PT and we resented the thought of being ordered into more mandatory exercise. We believed we were commissioned officers and had earned the privilege of being treated as such. Our objections were ignored and the Colonel insisted that his orders concerning PT were to be followed. We, the pilots in training, learned that the Colonel's effectiveness as a commander would be judged on the total number of flying hours we logged in training. Almost as a unit the pilots decided to reduce the number of hours each airplane was flyable. The ground crew (mechanics) serviced each airplane and pronounced it ready for flight. However, the pilot had the last say-so as to whether the plane was mechanically safe to fly.

The P-47 was controlled while taxiing to and from the runway by pressure on the brake pedals mounted above the rudder controls. During hot weather, which was common in Nebraska in the summer, the brakes on the P-47 overheated readily. When one brake overheats, it is impossible to control the airplane on the ground and using the one functioning brake would just cause the plane to go around in a circle. When a brake malfunction occurred, the pilot would contact the control tower by radio and report the malfunction, shut the engine off and wait for the tow vehicle to come and pull the plane to the hangar area. It was rather evident that many more brakes were overheating than usual, but the hot weather was blamed, and no comments to the contrary came from the pilots. The plane with the overheated brakes was parked until the brakes cooled enough to become functional again.

Normal procedures after making a cockpit check of all instruments was to taxi out to the end of the runway and just prior to moving onto the runway, brakes were applied and the engine was held at a steady RPM (revolutions per minute) to check the magnetos. The R-2800 was equipped with two sets of spark plugs for each cylinder. When the engine switch was fully on both magnetos both sets of spark plugs were firing. The switch was moved to the right (magneto) and the drop in RPM was noted. This procedure was repeated for the left magneto RPM check. If the drop was greater than 200 RPM while on either, right or left magneto, the pilot was justified in returning the plane to the hangar for a change of spark plugs. It was common knowledge among the pilots (and mechanics) that if a plane was taxied out to the runway with only one (right or left) magneto (and respective set of spark plugs) turned on, the remaining set of spark plugs would get fouled. During the RPM check at the end of the runway, the fouled set of plugs invariably dropped more than the 200 RPM limit and consequently, the pilot would bring the plane back to the hangar where the mechanics replaced the fouled plugs. For almost a week there was a significant increase in the number of P-47 airplanes that were being temporarily grounded with brake problems and spark plug changes. Grounded planes didn't log any flying time and the flying time per aircraft plummeted. To make a long story shorter, the Infantry Colonel was replaced by an Air Corps Colonel. The new Commanding Officer required no marching to the flight line and the required PT was defined as playing basketball in the gymnasium in our spare time. Almost immediately the number of pilot reported malfunctions of the P-47 aircraft decreased and the logged flying time per aircraft rose back to normal. It was the end of the only silent revolt I witnessed while on active duty.

While at Bruning Field I made some lasting friendships with several pilots: Tom McCaffrey (Mac),

Lowell Scales (L.D.), Earl Stenejhem (Jeem) and Donald St. Clare (Saint). Certainly there were others, Carl Gray, Bob Falconer, Don Deifke, Bob Eschweiler, Pete Harms, Warren Tyrell, Lee Tucker and several others whose names are not recalled. However, I and the four first mentioned, Mac, L.D., Jeem and Saint became close friends throughout the war and the years after. According to Mac, Jeem (Stenejhem) was the first to call me "Pop" after we were overseas a short while. The name caught on, and from then on I was known as "Pop" Zlaten. I guess I exhibited a fatherly concern, primarily for my four close comrades: Mac, Jeem, L. D. and Saint.

After flying the Jug (as the P-47 was often called) for several weeks, I began to be more comfortable during high speed maneuvers, which is the only way to truly learn an airplane's limitations and handling characteristics. On several occasions four or five pilots would get together in the air and follow the leader with the leader doing maneuvers to get the planes following off his tail. It was good training and a lot of fun. Being the leader was the most fun because you didn't have to anticipate the next move and you controlled the speed of the maneuvers. This exercise was called a "rat race", probably named by the combat pilots describing encounters with enemy aircraft. It was my turn to be number five in the follow the leader "rat race". The last position in line is the least desirable since each succeeding pilot has to do the exact maneuver performed by the pilot ahead of him. To keep from flying past the plane ahead each succeeding pilot does the identical maneuver at a slower speed than the preceding pilot. The maneuver in this case was an Immelmann (a roll out at the top of a loop). I could see each plane ahead of me slowing down a bit, and when I started the loop I felt I was going to be too slow at the top of the loop to complete a half roll. I was right, as I started the half roll at the top of the loop the P-47 stalled out for lack of sufficient speed and actually tumbled. Fortunately our rat race was above ten thousand feet in altitude and I had time to recover before running out of altitude. Tumbling a Thunderbolt fighter aircraft is not something that is done intentionally. The tumbling takes place rapidly and is disorienting. While I was moving the controls and reducing the throttle setting in order to recover from the unplanned behavior of the aircraft I lost several thousand feet of altitude and lost sight of my friends. I examined the P-47 for structural damage and seeing no apparent damage, I began looking for my friends whom I spotted high above me going in the opposite direction. I never did find out the exact gyrations the P-47 performed during the tumble, but I was convinced that the P-47 required a minimum speed to complete certain maneuvers satisfactorily.

Yes, there were many more memorable incidents while flying the P-47 fighter aircraft than there were during all of the previous cadet flight training. Flying a fighter aircraft is an inherently dangerous occupation, and this fact was confirmed by the number of casualties and near casualties that occurred during the training at Bruning Field. One incident in particular, which was over in a matter of seconds, caused me to lose my temper to such an extent that I wanted to physically beat up on the instructor on whose wing I was flying during a particular training mission. As part of our training, we flew joint training missions with B-17 heavy bombers from a training field in Kansas. The squadron of bombers flew over in close formation at about 20,000 feet and our assignment, as fighter pilots, was to attack the bomber formation. Of course no live ammunition was used by either the bombers or fighter aircraft. The gunners on the bombers activated cameras mounted on their guns while "fighting off" our attack. I was assigned to be a wing man for my instructor, who was a young red-headed First Lieutenant. I was to fly on his right wing as we made our diving pass on the bombers from 25,000 feet. We came down at the bombers at nearly five hundred miles per hour. At that speed we closed on the B-17's very rapidly. My red-headed instructor (I didn't remember his name and didn't care to) directed his dive to carry him just behind the left wing of a B-17. While he planned to fly close to the bomber, he forgot that I was right on his wing. Intent on diving close to the bomber, the instructor left no room for me to miss the bomber. If I held my course at close to 500 miles per hour I would crash right through the bomber just behind the wings! A micro-second decision was made and I moved the controls enough to fly my P-47 directly between two B-17 bombers flying in close formation. The realization that my thoughtless red-headed instructor had placed me and the bomber crew in a hazardous predicament made my temper rise to a boiling point. On landing, I was determined to find my instructor and "punch his lights out". The red-headed First Lieutenant landed ahead of me and he was nowhere to be found as I angrily searched for him and inquired as to his whereabouts. His quick disappearance from the flight line confirmed the fact he realized what a bone-headed stunt he had pulled. Fortunately for both of us I didn't learn of his whereabouts for several days and by that time I had cooled down enough to act in a rational manner. Did I actually dive through the bomber formation? Well, the Commanding General, who was aboard one of the B-17's, stated that "the fighter pilots were very aggressive and one pilot actually flew through the bomber formation". Little did he know that aggressiveness was not planned. Was the probability of a collision between an attacking fighter plane and a bomber a real danger?

A short time after my near miss, another P-47 pilot was not as fortunate as he crashed into a B-17 killing himself and several B-17 crew members, who were unable to parachute out of their disabled bomber.

Aerial And Ground Gunnery Training At Pierre, South Dakota

Our training at Bruning Field included two weeks of gunnery training at an airfield near Pierre, South Dakota. Several P-47's were permanently located at Pierre and every two weeks pilot trainees were flown to gunnery school in a C-47 transport plane. Gunnery school was divided into ground gunnery and aerial gunnery. Aerial gunnery practice was conducted over the Badlands (an almost inaccessible area of rough terrain west of Pierre). One late afternoon I was in a flight of four, led by an instructor, and we had just completed the day's aerial gunnery practice. Aerial gunnery consisted of firing six of the eight wing-mounted 50 caliber machine guns (two machine guns were left on the ground) at a target towed at the end of a steel cable pulled by another P-47. The belted ammunition in each aircraft was painted with a different color. Hits left a colored ring around the hole in the canvas target, and credit for hits was given to the pilot with the matching colored ammunition. At any rate, during this particular mission we had used up all our ammunition and returned to the field where the hits were to be counted after the tow pilot dropped the tow target. The Commanding Officer at the gunnery school inspected the target and discovered that the target had not sustained a single hit. The instructor, who had led the flight, was preparing to leave for Pierre where he had a date that night. However, the C.O., who was disgusted by our poor gunnery, had other ideas. He ordered the planes refueled and the guns reloaded and we were all ordered to fly another aerial gunnery mission. The instructor who led the previous scoreless mission was already late for his date in town, so he was in a hurry to get the mission completed. He said, "I want everyone joined up in formation before I circle the field". Following the instructor, we took off one by one and, you guessed it, I was last in line to take off. As I was getting ready to roll down the runway I could see that the instructor had already made his turn and I would have to hustle to join up before he headed for the gunnery range. I lined up on the runway, set the brakes, gave the engine full throttle, released the brakes and rapidly accelerated down the runway. The plane reached flying speed rapidly, I lifted off the runway and started to turn and climb. Since I was in a hurry to join up, as I was instructed, I made my turn long before the end of the runway and my flight path carried me directly over the firehouse right after take off. The turbo supercharger was streaming black smoke as I flew over the firehouse. Unbeknownst to me, the firemen, anticipating a crash, bolted out of the firehouse with their fire truck. In the meantime I was hustling to catch up to the formation heading for the gunnery range. The P-47 I was flying was performing normally and the black smoke from the turbo was just a temporary condition. We made our gunnery passes on the target in turn and suddenly the tow cable was hit and severed by the fifty caliber bullets; and the target drifted down into the Badlands where it probably would not be recovered. We all headed back to the field and upon landing everyone insisted that they scored numerous hits on the target. Since there was no target to check, the C.O. shook his head and waved us on to town for the evening.

Ground gunnery was also interesting but more dangerous to the pilot. The eight-foot by eight-foot target was mounted on the ground and each pilot fired while diving toward the target. The dangerous part was getting target fixation while firing. You became so intent on hitting the target that you waited too long to pull up and came dangerously close to the ground. The P-47 was a heavy aircraft, and when you pulled up from a gunnery run, the attitude of the plane changed, but the flight path continued for a split second as the plane mushed toward the ground. On one occasion I was reprimanded for diving too low by the instructor observing, who stated that I almost hit the target with the turbo, which protruded below the plane near the tail section. His concern, because of low pull outs from gunnery runs, was justified as several days later one of the pilots on a ground gunnery run pulled up too late and was fatally injured as his plane hit the ground. After gunnery training was over, we were all flown back to Bruning Field.

One of the last training missions at Bruning Field was a low level cross country flight to be flown by individual aircraft at an altitude of about 200 feet (or less). Most pilots had done some low level flying, other than ground gunnery, but it wasn't approved by the Training Command. An altitude of 200 feet was specified for the training mission to safely clear tall trees, water towers and high voltage power lines. Like most pilots, I relished the idea of flying at low level in a fighter plane. The lower the flight the greater the sensation of speed. We were to fly a triangular shaped course going northwest first to Grand Island, Nebraska, then east to Columbus, Nebraska and then south back to Bruning Field, a distance of about 200 miles. In a P-47 flight time, including takeoff and landing, would be a little over one hour. Prior to takeoff we were informed that a thunderstorm system covered a large area with rainfall east of Grand Island. Those of us flying the training mission were expected to handle a little rough weather, since we were all declared proficient in instrument flying, and the

P-47 was a stable aircraft in all weather. I took off and climbed to about a hundred feet. I passed over a farm yard where the cattle started to run in the pasture and the chickens flew helter-skelter as I flew by. As I arrived at Grand Island I was flying in a rainstorm which reduced visibility to less than a mile. I turned toward Columbus and immediately flew into more rain and reduced visibility. Below me I could see the highway running between Grand Island and Columbus. As the rain grew more intense and visibility decreased, I dropped lower to just above tree top level. I could see the automobiles on the highway below me as I swiftly passed by them. As I glanced at a farmhouse I was passing over, I noticed that a young lad had run out into the farmyard in the rain. I used to do that as a boy when I heard a plane fly over during a rainstorm. I quickly decided to slow down and circle the farm yard and wave at the boy on the ground who was waving at me. My act of recognition toward the boy, who had run out into the rain to wave, made me feel good as I swung back on course following the highway. The rain continued and visibility remained poor. The next thing I knew I was looking down into the second story windows of buildings in Columbus, Nebraska! Over the radio I heard that three other pilots, who were flying on the edge of the storm to the north, decided to fly farther east to get around the storm. Visibility was so poor I decided that flying by visual contact was too risky, so I went on instruments, climbed to 1500 feet in altitude and turned on course toward Bruning Army Air Field. I flew on instruments in the rain clouds for about twenty minutes before I broke out of the storm. In another fifteen minutes I landed at Bruning Field right on schedule. Total flight time was one hour and thirty minutes. I was glad to get some practice instrument flying. The three pilots who skirted the storm discovered that the storm area was more widespread than expected. The three pilots landed after three hours and thirty minutes in the air, and with nearly empty fuel tanks.

Training was over and Special Order 204 was issued, transferring the Class of 5-29-44 (the class that had just finished transitional training in P-47's) to Harding Field, Baton Rouge, Louisiana. I checked the orders and all of my classmates and friends were listed on the order, but my name was not on the list. Several of the pilots were being assigned to Bruning Field as instructors, but I had not desired to be an instructor and no one had discussed such an assignment with me. All I knew was that my friends were leaving and my name was not on the list to go with them. I hurried over to Headquarters to find out why my name was not on the orders for Harding Field. It was as I expected, with a last name starting with the letter "Z" it was not uncommon to have your records lost, be left off of orders and end up temporarily unassigned. Additional orders were issued adding my name to the list going to Harding Field. I was relieved to be going with my friends, but I did have a thought that staying on as an instructor for three months might be a good duty assignment. We boarded the train for Baton Rouge and the evening of the second day's journey someone picked up a newspaper during a stop. The headlines indicated that a C-47 transport plane, carrying instructor pilots and mechanics from Bruning Field to the gunnery school at Pierre, South Dakota, crashed during a thunderstorm and all twenty-eight persons aboard were killed. Among the instructor pilots on board the ill-fated C-47 were several members of our class who had just been assigned as flight instructors. At that moment I felt fortunate to be aboard the train heading for Harding Field with my friends.

CHAPTER FIVE
Destination Overseas

The second assignment to Harding Field, Louisiana was for less than two weeks as we received inoculations for various diseases, were fitted with flight gear, such as oxygen masks and parachutes and, last but not least, made and signed our last wills. For some it proved to be a last will and testament. From Harding Field it was on the train again as we traveled up the east coast to Camp Kilmer, New Jersey. Camp Kilmer was an Embarkation Point for overseas troop movement. During our stay, half of the men in our contingent were allowed to go to New York City one night and the second half were to go the next night. I was in the group to go the first night, but my friends were not on the list, so I elected to wait and go the second night. However, there was no second night, as everyone was put on alert and we were transported to the harbor in New York City. There we were loaded onto a luxury liner, converted into a troop ship for the duration of the war. The ship was named the Columbia, or more correctly "Colombia" since it was of South American registry. Quarters were crowded and sleeping bunks were stacked three high. Meals for officers were served in the dining room, where the menu was a far cry from the food served aboard the ship when it was a tourist luxury liner. Powdered eggs and mutton. Mutton comes from sheep that are old. The meat was tough and unappetizing. After several days of mutton and more mutton we began to gag on it.

Our ship was part of a convoy of nearly a hundred ships. The convoy consisted of troop ships, tankers, freighters and destroyer escorts. It was impossible to see all the ships in the convoy since they were spaced over a wide expanse of ocean. The bad part about a convoy, madc up of several types of ships, is that the convoy can move only at the top speed of the slowest ship. The German U-boat threat had been countered with some success by the Navy and aircraft flying submarine patrol; however, ships were still being sunk by the enemy submarines. Our slow progress was especially disturbing to the pilots on board who were used to moving from one place to another in a hurry. We could see the oil tankers off our port side (left side to you landlubbers). Due to their full load, the tankers rode low in the water and large waves occasionally splashed over the tankers. This was normal for tankers, but the disturbing part was that we could see that several P-47's were lashed to the decks of each tanker. We kept thinking that we would be flying some of those P-47's and the sight of ocean waves breaking over the top of the airplanes was disconcerting. We were told that the airplanes were adequately protected and would weather the sea voyage satisfactorily.

Near the Azores we ran into foul weather and the waves were higher than we had seen so far. At times the oil tankers, with the P-47's strapped on deck, were completely lost from sight. After a day or so of stormy weather, the sea became calm and the convoy resumed its normal speed. As we drew near to the British Isles, the weather deteriorated and tension increased as we were nearing U-boat Alley. We later learned that at least two freighters located on the outer edges of our convoy were sunk by German submarines. Additional casualties were prevented by quick action of destroyers escorting the convoy.

After fourteen days at sea we docked at Liverpool, England. Within a few hours we disembarked and boarded a train that took us to Scotland, where we spent less than two weeks. There didn't seem to be any organized training while we were there and we had lots of free time with nowhere to go. I believe we were in some type of holding station. We were being kept there until there was space for us at an airfield from which replacements were sent to various combat units in either the Eighth or Ninth Air Force. Such a place was Atcham Field near Wolverhampton and Shrewsbury, England, which turned out to be our next station.

Facilities at Atcham were all dispersed around the field so that none of the buildings were clustered close together. Most of the buildings were hastily constructed Quonset huts. The Quonsets were also used as quarters for the personnel on the field. To facilitate movement from one area of the field to another, bicycles were issued to us and they were the main mode of transportation. In the evening Mac (McCaffrey) and I would pedal to one of several Pubs located in the area. After watching the locals participate in their game of darts, and after a glass of "bitters" we would pedal our way back to the airfield in the pitch black darkness. Blackout was strictly enforced ever since the first German air raids over England. One glass of "bitters" (English beer) was usually enough since the beer must have received its name from its taste.

Our stay at Atcham was in September and part of October, 1944. We had not participated in any flying activity since we left Bruning, Nebraska in the later part of July. At Atcham we began flying again as the weather permitted. The weather over England changes rapidly. We would take off under favorable weather conditions and in a space of several minutes we would be advised by radio to return to base. The radio message would start a rush of P-47's returning to the field to land before the field became socked in. Records indicate that a large percentage of losses, of planes and crew flying missions, was due to mishaps caused by unfavorable weather conditions. Flying by instruments often became necessary during our training flights. On one occasion I was barely able to land before the field was completely obscured by low lying clouds. A friend of mine who was flying at the time was unable to see the field due to the quick moving clouds and rain. He lost radio contact and in the overcast he lost his bearings and was not heard from again. Since no crash of a P-47 was reported on the Island, we presumed he flew over the water, ran out of fuel and disappeared in the ocean or the English Channel.

On another occasion Jeem (Stenejhem) and I were flying our P-47's above the overcast and decided to let down through the clouds and find our way back to Atcham. As we broke out of the overcast we found ourselves in the midst of a large number of gas filled barrage balloons, which were a part of defenses against German bombing raids. These balloons were secured to the ground by cables, and were tethered at different altitudes to make low level flight extremely hazardous. We were maneuvering in and around the balloons, trying to avoid becoming entangled in their cables. After a short time of courting disaster with the balloons, we pulled up and climbed back through the clouds and made our letdown in a safer area.

Each pilot had to fly a two-man training mission where one day you were the wing man and the next day you flew as the element leader (two-plane element). It was my day to be the element leader as the two of us flew around the area. My wing man, as was expected of him, stayed close to me for over an hour. I didn't do any surprise maneuvers to make life miserable for my wing man. By plane-to-plane radio communications I informed my wing man we would make a normal landing approach consisting of a shallow dive over the end of the runway, pull up in a climbing turn, drop the landing gear and complete the 180-degree turn by landing on the first one-fourth of the runway. I landed normally, cleared rapidly to the far end of the runway, and as I turned off onto the taxi strip, I looked back to check on my wing man. I was a bit surprised that there was no P-47 following me down the runway. However, I was not concerned, since I figured he didn't like his first approach and was going around to make another landing approach. As I parked my airplane, a mechanic told me a P-47 had just crashed at the end of the runway! I commandeered a Jeep and driver and we sped to the approach end of the runway. As we neared the end of the runway, I could see that my wing man had belly landed (wheels up) about a hundred yards short of the runway. The crash crew was already at the scene, and as we approached the crash site I looked about for the pilot of the airplane. I spotted him, standing near the disabled P-47 nervously puffing on a cigarette. I asked him if he was all right and he replied that he was O.K. Then I asked, "What happened?" Evidently as he pulled up from the shallow dive on approach, prior to dropping his landing gear, the engine of the P-47 quit. When the engine stopped he was too far from the runway to try to make an emergency wheels down landing on the runway. Wisely he left the landing gear up and belly landed in the field near the end of the runway. The ruggedness of the P-47 was demonstrated as the airplane skidded through a piled up rock wall, common in this area of England, just missed the MP's (Military Police) shack and came to a stop. Except for some badly frayed nerves, my wing man was uninjured.

As we neared the end of our stay at Atcham, an announcement was made that there would be a list of available Fighter Groups and respective Fighter Squadrons that needed replacement pilots. These needs were to be filled by those of us who were presently stationed at Atcham Field. The list was posted and my close friends, Stenejhem,

St. Clare, Scales, McCaffrey and I decided to pick a Fighter Group that needed at least five replacement pilots. As we read the replacement needs of the various Fighter Groups, we noted that the 373rd Fighter Group needed fourteen replacement pilots. We figured if we put our names in for the 373rd we would have a good chance of staying together. Our hopes were realized and the five of us were assigned to report to the 373rd Fighter Group.

Training was completed at Atcham where in addition to flying the P-47, we had been instructed by experienced fighter pilots on the hazards of combat flying. We were also introduced to procedures, learned from experience, that would increase our chances of survival while flying combat missions. From Atcham we were transported by rail to a staging area near Southampton, England.

We stayed one night in tents that were filled with army cots to the point that there was no room to walk between the cots. We only had to put up with these crowded conditions one night and the next day we climbed aboard trucks that hauled us to another staging area closer to the port of Southampton. Our stay at this location also lasted only one night, as the next day we boarded an LST (Landing Ship Tank). In addition to the human cargo of replacement pilots, the LST was loaded to capacity with tanks and military trucks. The ship did not leave port until darkness had fallen over the English Channel. The threat of German U-boats was being taken seriously and sailing across the Channel in daylight was still hazardous. The LST had been at sea only a short time before we were introduced to the rough waters of the English Channel. The LST rolled and pitched continuously. Serving of "chow" was announced and we decided to at least see what was on the menu for the evening. Canned wieners and beans were being served. Most of us decided to pass on dinner considering what was being served and the tossing about of the LST by the rough sea. The "cooks" told us that they couldn't prepare a more savory meal due to the rough sea. Which was just as well since we probably wouldn't have eaten anyway. We did finally fall asleep in our bunks after midnight. When we were awakened early the next morning, we found that the LST was at Omaha Beach. Omaha Beach was where our troops had landed and fought while we were still at Bruning Field, and at other training fields in the States. The moveable bow of the LST was dropped to form a ramp to the shore, except the ramp didn't quite reach the beach. The trucks and tanks were being unloaded and made their way through the shallow water to the beach. Then it was our turn to wade ashore. We were thankful there was no enemy fire coming our way as was the case only a few weeks before. When on shore, our "glorious leaders" decided we would walk to the airstrip which someone said was down the road aways. Pilots were meant to fly, not walk, and after walking until almost noon, there was a unanimity of protest against continuing our march. At last Army trucks caught up to us and transported us the remainder of the distance to Airstrip A-9. Our truck passed through St. Lo, France, where we saw a completely destroyed town that had been bombed and shelled by artillery. Bombed and shelled, first by American forces, then by Germans as they retreated. We were beginning to get the picture of devastation caused by war.

A-9 was tent city again, but the tents were much less crowded than our last tent city. Our days were spent loafing around our tents. Excursions into the countryside were discouraged due to unexploded mortar shells and enemy mines still scattered throughout the terrain. After four days of semi-confinement to our tent area, C-47 transport planes landed at the airstrip and we were flown to Orly Field near

Paris. Paris had been spared the devastation of other cities in Europe, primarily because the Commanding General in the city had refused to carry out Hitler's order to destroy the city before retreating toward Germany. The German army pulled out of Paris before the Allied troops arrived and there was no battle for possession of the city. From Orly Field we rode in trucks to a large building in the city that was our temporary quarters. The building was jam packed with cots and was so crowded that cots were in the hallways. In retrospect some of our tent city quarters were more desirable. But this was Paris and Jeem, Mac, St. Clare, L.D. and I were still together and we were anxious to explore the sights of the city. Our arrival was late afternoon and by the time we were settled and free to go look around about the only places open were the nightclubs of Paris. After walking around for several hours we selected a club we wanted to go into, but found there was standing room only. Between the numerous servicemen in Paris, and the liberated Parisians, most of the clubs were full to capacity. We had selected the well known Bal Tabrin, which had a stage that was hydraulically raised and lowered. The maitre'd who stood at the locked gate informed us there was absolutely no room in the night club. Since none of us smoked, we all saved our allotment of American cigarettes, some of which we had on our person. Lucky Strike, Chesterfield and Camels were among the favored brands. The maitre'd had turned down our offer of several hundred French francs to find us a table inside, but when we started to barter with packs of American cigarettes, he couldn't resist. The maitre'd asked us to wait a few minutes and disappeared into the night club. In a short time he was back and said he had set up a table for us next to the stage. Sure enough, he led us to a table that was closer to the stage than any of the surrounding tables. For the price of a half dozen packs of American cigarettes, we were able to watch the performers from a ringside or more appropriately, a stage side seat. Along with the customary cancan dancers, there were jugglers, magicians, acrobats and trapeze performers. One couldn't help but think that only a few weeks before these entertainers were performing for the occupying enemy troops, albeit was a command performance.

Our sojourn to the night clubs was over early in the evening as the clubs closed down before midnight. The next day, Sunday, I wanted to find a Catholic church to attend. Someone suggested the Church of the Madeleine, which was several miles away. I set out on foot in the general direction of the majestic structure, easily visible from a distance. After over an hour's walk I came to the steps leading to the magnificent church which was constructed during the time of Napoleon. As I started up the stairs to the church I noticed that a large number of people were coming out of the church. I looked at my watch and noticed it was nearly eleven o'clock and I figured it had taken so long to walk the long distance from our quarters that I was too late to attend a complete Mass. As I entered the enormous structure, which appeared larger on the inside than it did from the outside, I wasn't quite sure what was taking place and walked hesitantly. A person just entering the church understood my predicament and motioned for me to follow him. What was taking place was that Mass was being said at six or seven altars at staggered times. Consequently, anyone entering was sure to find a service that was just beginning. It was a new experience for me. I marveled at the beauty of the church structure and its grandeur, certainly befitting a temple of worship to our God.

CHAPTER SIX

Joining The 373rd Fighter Bomber Group

Our stay in Paris was short and in a couple of days we were being transported by truck to Rheims, France, where the 373rd Fighter Bomber Group was located. Along the highway there were many burned out German military vehicles that were destroyed by the advancing Allied Forces. It wasn't hard to imagine that many of the wrecked and disabled vehicles had fallen prey to the strafing of P-47 fighter aircraft.

The 373rd Group occupied an airfield that had been used by the Luftwaffe and had been liberated by Allied Forces. Remnants of German aircraft were scattered around the airfield. An abandoned Messerschmitt-109 was behind the hangar and inside the hangar was a Focke-Wulf-190 that was intact. A Frenchman who had been a mechanic at the airfield told us the FW-190 was abandoned by the Germans, during their retreat, because the engine needed repair. He also said that he subsequently had repaired the engine and the FW-190 was flyable. None of the pilots in the 373rd Fighter Group were allowed to attempt a flight in the German fighter. It was feared that, before they retreated, the Germans had booby-trapped the plane so it would explode if anyone tried to fly it. Consequently, we never found out if the German FW-190 was airworthy. The P-47's of the 373rd Fighter Group were dispersed around the airfield so that, in the event of a German air raid upon the airfield, there would be no concentration of P-47's and losses during such a raid would be minimized.

Finally we were with the Fighter Group in which we would be flying combat missions. There were no barracks at the airfield; as a result pilots were quartered in several large houses in Rheims itself, approximately three miles from the airfield. We wondered who owned the houses, but that was academic, what the military forces required, the military forces occupied.

One of the benefits of finally reaching our assigned Fighter Group was that our mail was able to catch up with us. The letters from loved ones at home had been accumulating during our travels from Scotland, through England, across the Channel, and into France. "Mail Call" was a bonanza of overdue letters for all of us replacement pilots. I recall arranging the letters in chronological order by postmark date so I could read the oldest letter first. The letters were read and re-read until all of the news, expressions of love and concerns were memorized.

A month had passed since we had last flown P-47's in England, and most of us were beginning to feel the need to fly again to keep up our flying skills. When spare aircraft were available, we were allowed several hours of flying time in the near vicinity of our airdrome.

In the meantime, since we left Scotland, the Allied Forces had rapidly pushed back the German Army and once again the front lines were too far from the airfield occupied by the 373rd Fighter Group. To reduce flying time to and from the front, the 373rd Fighter Group was moving. The move was to an airfield southeast of Brussels, Belgium, near the small village of Jodoigne (officially the location was called La Culet, Belgium). The airfield consisted of a single asphalt runway; however, it was only five minutes from the front lines, permitting us to make deeper penetration into the enemy territory without auxiliary fuel tanks. In addition, the 373rd could respond quickly to a request from the ground forces for aerial support during a push against the German forces or during a defensive battle due to a German counter attack. Housing for the pilots was in a large chateau about four miles from the airfield. The chateau was large enough for all the pilots from all three squadrons, and a large room on the ground floor served as a mess hall. After briefing on the details of the day's mission, pilots were transported to the airfield in covered Army four-by-four trucks, which were smaller than the conventional Army trucks. The four-by-four trucks were faster and easier to handle.

It was now the first week of November, 1944, and none of the fourteen replacement pilots had flown on a bonafide combat mission. Everyone of us wondered who would be the first to fly a combat mission. Most of the replacement pilots expressed their eagerness to fly combat, but one or two wanted to be first. Almost unexpectedly one of our group of fourteen was scheduled for the morning mission. The new replacement, with the distinction of being the first of our group of fourteen to fly a mission, took off with eleven veteran pilots and headed toward the front. The rest of us awaited the return of the planes from the mission over enemy territory. After about two hours the planes were sighted approaching the airfield. One by one they landed and when they were all down but one, we inquired about the missing plane. "He didn't make it" was the reply we received. "Who was it?", we asked. "It was the new replacement", we were told. That was our welcome to the real world of combat flying. Only one of our group of replacement pilots was on that first mission and he didn't return. He wanted to be first to fly a combat mission and he was first to go, but he didn't even have a chance to come back and tell us about it. It was a sobering experience for the rest of us new pilots. We would all get our chance to find out what it was like to fly with the 373rd Fighter Group on missions against the enemy.

The 373rd Fighter Group was made up of three squadrons, the 410th, 411th, and the 412th (I was assigned to the 412th squadron). Each squadron was usually made up of three flights of four aircraft. Each flight was assigned a color: red, blue or yellow. A flight of four consisted of the flight leader, his wing man, position number two, the element leader, position number three, and his wing man, position number four.

For a squadron mission, thirteen P-47's were readied with fuel, ammunition and bombs. The extra plane was called a "spare" and the pilot of the spare aircraft would accompany the squadron to the front lines and would replace any plane that would abort the mission (return to base) due to mechanical problems. If no plane aborted the mission and the target was deep in enemy territory, the pilot of the "spare" would return to the base and would not get credit for a combat mission. However, if the mission was scheduled for dive bombing and strafing enemy positions near the frontlines (close support mission), the pilot of the spare would often join the action.

On rare occasions, during maximum effort, a Group mission was scheduled, consisting of three squadrons of twelve aircraft each, for a total of thirty-six aircraft.

A day or so after the no return of the first replacement pilot to fly a mission, it was my turn to fly my first mission. I was assigned to fly as wing man for the element leader, Louie Brewer, in Blue Flight, which made my position Blue Four. Blue Flight was given the assignment of flying top cover for the other two flights. As top cover we did not carry any bombs, but were to fly above the rest of the squadron and protect them from any enemy aircraft that might appear in the area, while they proceeded to dive bomb and strafe their target. We had all been briefed to expect German antiaircraft fire, which everyone referred to as "flak". It is said that the word "flak" was derived from the German word fliegerabwerkanone. Although, to me, the derivation was not clear; nevertheless, the word "flak" was to become one of the most used words in our daily conversation.

Flying top cover, I presumed, was a reasonably safe way to introduce new pilots to flying combat missions. As we crossed the front line, the German antiaircraft gunners greeted us with several burst of heavy flak (flak encountered above 10,000 feet was usually large caliber, of 88mm and/or 105mm and termed “heavy flak”, below 10,000 feet smaller caliber, 20mm and 40mm flack combined with heavy flak was encountered). Our target for the day was several hundred miles deep into Germany and as we made our way to the target area we flew through several areas where flak was not encountered. As we neared the target, several bursts of flak appeared ahead of us. At first the heavy flak did not burst close to our flight flying top cover. But as we orbited over the red and yellow flights below, the heavy flak bursts became more numerous. The flight leader changed our course and altitude about every 25 seconds (to me it didn’t seem often enough), which made it more difficult for the radar-controlled guns to estimate our position for the next round of flak. After what seemed like a very long time, the two lower flights joined together and headed back to the front lines. Our top cover flight turned with them and the squadron began the hour long flight to the front lines. The squadron leader avoided area flak defenses until we reached the front lines where the German flak gunners took parting shots at us.

The radar controlled heavy flak batteries usually contained four guns, and when the battery fired, four black puffs of smoke, in a box pattern, indicated where the antiaircraft shells exploded, which was usually at the altitude we were flying.

We finally reached our home airstrip and all planes landed safely. My first mission was over after more that three hours in the air. This first mission proved to be one of the longest that I would fly. I was aware of the fact that bomber crews sometimes flew eight to ten hour missions and I was glad that our missions were shorter. I felt relieved when my first mission was over and I didn't get hit by flak. I was hoping my next mission would also be top cover. The very next day I flew my second mission, on which we all carried a one thousand pound bomb which we delivered to our target. Our airstrip was quite short, and loaded with ammunition, fuel and bombs; the heavy P-47 required every foot of the runway to become airborne.

In this narrative, it is not my intention to describe in detail the missions I flew, and I elaborate on some of the more interesting events. However, I do not mean to imply that some of the missions were insignificant. Every mission was significant in that there is an inherent element of risk in all missions, especially combat missions.

Aircraft at our airfield were parked in their own respective places in a dispersed manner to make them less vulnerable to an enemy air attack. At the start of a mission, each pilot taxied his plane to the single air strip for take off in the assigned sequence. It was impossible to look over the nose of the P-47, so taxiing was a slow process as each pilot zig zagged down the taxi strip to make sure he was a safe distance from the plane in front. There was ample time during taxiing, and it certainly was an appropriate time, for prayers for a safe return from the combat mission about to be flown. I am certain I am not the only pilot who started a mission with a prayer on his lips. Some of the crew chiefs and their crew, who made certain the planes were mechanically ready to fly, often prayed for the safe return of their pilot.

All wars result in destruction, misery, pain and inhumane acts by those involved in combat. By its very nature war is based on inflicting as much destruction, of lives and upon the physical ability of the enemy to wage war, as is required to make the enemy cease all conflict and surrender. These cold, unfeeling words do not begin to describe the human pain and misery that is suffered, not only by the fighting forces, but more so by the civilian population of the nations upon whose soil the evil forces of war are daily unleashed.

As pilots involved in conflict, we understood the grim realities of war, but this understanding and natural revulsion to such violence had to be subdued, pushed aside and not dwelt upon, so that we could carry out our assigned mission.

During some of the missions that were the most difficult all planes and pilots returned safely, and during some of the supposedly easier missions , aircraft were lost or damaged and/or aircraft and pilots were lost. I kept a record of missions flown and wrote brief comments describing the mission and opposition encountered. The following are some of my recorded comments:

Diary Of Missions Flown, 1944

MISSION 1, NOVEMBER 4: Flew Blue Four position in top cover flight on a deep penetration flight into Nazi Germany. My first encounter with hostile antiaircraft fire (flak). Intensity of flak was moderate. All aircraft returned to base. Mission lasted over three hours, one of the longest I flew.

MISSION 2, NOVEMBER 5: Dive bombing mission west of the Rhine River carrying a 1,000 lb. bomb.

MISSION 3, NOVEMBER 8: Fighter sweep mission, with extra fuel in belly tank, carrying no bombs. Flown east of the Rhine River. Objective: enemy aircraft and targets of opportunity on the ground. No enemy aircraft encountered.

MISSION 4, NOVEMBER 16: Bad weather had kept our planes grounded for a week. Today we carried three 500 lb. bombs and dive bombed between the Roer and Rhine Rivers in support of ground troops driving toward the Rhine. Weather was bad and flak was heavy and accurate, and we suffered the loss of a squadron leader.

MISSION 5, NOVEMBER 19: Dive bombing enemy positions near front lines, carried two 500 lb. bombs.

MISSION 6, NOVEMBER 19: Flew in top cover flight on dive bombing mission near front. It was my second mission of the day as a result of intensified action by ground forces to reach the Rhine River. Encountered accurate, heavy flak.

MISSION 7, NOVEMBER 20: Flew in the top cover flight second day in a row. Encountered heavy flak over Duren.

MISSION 8, NOVEMBER 21: A late afternoon mission where the 412th Squadron escorted a squadron of B-26 bombers, encountered only two bursts of flak as the bombers attracted most of the flak. All aircraft returned. For P-47 fighter pilots used to flying dive bombing missions, a bomber escort mission was a welcome diversion. Landed at home base after sunset.

MISSION 9, NOVEMBER 25: Today's mission was a three-squadron group mission planned as a deep penetration armed reconnaissance. All thirty-six aircraft carried two

500 lb. bombs. The target: a railroad yard and an unfortunate train caught in the railroad yard. The mission was longer than usual and took over three hours.

MISSION 10, NOVEMBER 26: Dive bombed a strategic road junction with bombs armed with six hour delay fuses. The objective was to deny the enemy the use of this area.

MISSION 11, NOVEMBER 28: On this day, it was my turn to fly the spare aircraft. Before the squadron reached the front lines, Red Three aborted the mission due to mechanical problems and I filled in as Red Three. We dive bombed a town in a close support mission and encountered light flak that was the most intense I had experienced to date.

MISSION 12, NOVEMBER 30: This was the second escort mission for me as the 412th squadron flew cover for a squadron of B-26 medium bombers. My notation indicated that we experienced no flak of any kind, a rare occurrence.

MISSION 13, DECEMBER 1: Flew in the top cover flight for a group mission; encountered a moderate amount of flak.

MISSION 14, DECEMBER 3: Top cover two missions in a row, this time for a squadron strength mission. Experienced near misses by heavy flak, as the explosions were close enough to be clearly heard above the ever present engine noise. The mission had special significance, as I was singularly involved in saving a pilot with whom I flew as wing man, and on alternate missions he flew as my wing man. We trusted each other and enjoyed flying together. We continued the element and wing man trade off relationship until someone discovered that we were two experienced pilots flying each other's wing, and decided to give us each a new replacement pilot as wing man. From that day on, I never had the same comfortable feeling on a mission as I did with Lt. Harris flying my wing and I on his wing. Harris was from Paducah, Kentucky, and we called him the "Duke of Paducah".

As we circled our home base, we made our approach for landing. Harris was immediately ahead of me and as he eased his P-47 to the runway, the left wheel of his landing gear hit the end of the runway and snapped completely off the landing strut, leaving Harris with one wheel. He must have realized he had made a poor approach and decided to go on around and make another approach. I had witnessed what had occurred and instead of landing, I pushed the throttle forward to catch up with Duke before he tried to land with one wheel missing. Someone who unknowingly lands with one wheel would end up cartwheeling the aircraft at over one hundred miles per hour, with a high probability of being fatally injured. As Duke came around for his second landing approach, I flew my P-47 across his path, crowding him off the runway. At the same time I was waving him away from the runway. In the meantime, the flight controller, in the control tower was trying to communicate with Duke over the radio. The impact that knocked the wheel off undoubtedly damaged his radio since he could not hear any of the radio transmission from the control tower, and his transmission into his microphone was not audible. The shouting and swearing over the radio by one of the group leaders on the ground contributed nothing worthwhile to the situation. Unaware of the condition of his plane's landing gear, Harris came in for a another attempt to land and once again, I crowded him off the runway. By this time he guessed that something was wrong. I gradually maneuvered my P-47 within a few feet of his. I was hoping he would be able to read my lips, or interpret my gestures and become aware of his situation. As we flew around the field in close formation, he spoke to me over the radio, and probably due to the nearness of our two planes, I could hear him. When I asked him if he could hear me, he acknowledged affirmatively. I told him about the condition of the damaged landing gear and instructed him to retract the landing gear and make a belly landing alongside the runway (so as not to block the runway being used by returning aircraft). These instructions met with the approval of the senior officers of the group. Lt. Harris made a safe belly landing and when we met after I landed, he expressed his gratitude for my actions. I was thankful I was able to save Duke from an accident that could have cost him his life. He confessed that at one time during the episode he wondered about my sanity because of my repetitive disruption of his attempts to land his aircraft.

MISSION 15, DECEMBER 4: On this day the squadron dive bombed railroad yards near Koln (Cologne). I noted that my bombs had destroyed two barracks at the edge of the railroad yards. Normally when pulling off a dive bomb run, the pilot is too busy trying to avoid the flak and the results of the individual's bombing are not observed; however, on this occasion I was able to see the results.

MISSION 16, DECEMBER 11: After being grounded by bad weather conditions, our mission was to dive bomb a wooded area near the front lines, southeast of Duren, which had been a spot where the Germans stubbornly resisted the Allies' advance. During these close support missions we were normally in radio contact with a pilot who was on the ground and served as a local coordinator between ground forces and air forces. We were informed that the target area would be marked by red smoke and proceeded to dive bomb the marked area. The ground controller requested us to strafe the area. Dive bombing was a risky business, but strafing was more so, as we had to dive close to the ground and fire our eight 50 caliber machine guns at the target on the ground. On a strafing pass, the aircraft is vulnerable to light flack and small arms fire from the ground. After we made three strafing passes we were released to return to base.

MISSION 17, DECEMBER 15: Flew the spare during start of the mission and filled in for Blue Three who had mechanical problems. Extremely low clouds prevented completion of the mission as planned and our bombs, fitted with long delay fuses, were dropped through the overcast in the Cologne-Duseldorf area. Heavy flak was encountered by Red and Yellow flights, but Blue flight encountered little flak.

MISSION 18, DECEMBER 17: On this day the sky was overcast as we flew towards our target. While still several miles from target, two enemy Focke-Wulf 190's broke out of the overcast about one hundred yards from my right wing. If the two FW 190's had, by chance, let down behind me, I might not be writing this book. As soon as the FW 190 pilots saw the squadron of P-47's, they turned and went full speed back into Germany. At the same time we jettisoned our bombs and belly tanks and several of us chased after the fleeing German pilots. We were not surprised to see the enemy aircraft since the pilots who had flown the morning mission had engaged several German fighter aircraft. During the morning mission three enemy aircraft were shot down and one of ours was lost, but the pilot parachuted safely on friendly territory. The two FW 190 pilots we were chasing knew that they would be leading us deeper and deeper into Germany; and we would be using up our fuel at a rapid rate while pursuing them at full throttle. We were unable to catch up to them and eventually decided to return to base, since our bombs were gone and we were low on fuel. In the meantime, clouds had dropped down and flying below the clouds would make us prime targets for enemy flak. I began climbing into the cloud cover with another P-47 flying on my wing. Flying a fairly straight course on instruments could be dangerous, as we found out. While in the overcast, flak burst near us and bounced our planes. The German radar had tracked us and we knew that more flak was on the way. The P-47 on my wing disappeared to my left in the overcast and I turned sharply to the right. By turning sharply I tumbled my gyroscope and my artificial horizon! My airspeed was climbing and my altimeter indicated a rapid loss of altitude! I was in a rapid downward spiral and needed to correct the attitude of my plane or I would hit the ground. Instrument flying had become second nature in the bad weather that occurred frequently in Western Europe. Flying strictly on instruments, I stopped the spiraling and reduced my airspeed as I maneuvered into a shallow dive. As I came out of the overcast at an altitude of about one thousand feet, I was greeted by a barrage of antiaircraft fire! No wonder, I had broken out of the overcast over the middle of Cologne, which was heavily defended by flak guns. I pulled back up into the overcast just enough to be invisible from the ground, but I still had enough visibility to see the ground and could avoid flying on instruments. Since the light flak gunners couldn't see me, I was rid of the light flak. I flew toward home base in a zigzag course to avoid the radar controlled heavy flak batteries which did not let up in their efforts to shoot me down. Back at home base I was

A visitor from the night, a Royal Air Force bomber, makes an emergency landing at the 373rd airstrip after suffering damage during a night raid on Germany.

St. Clare, "Pop" Zlaten, and McCaffery.

relieved to learn that the pilot who was flying on my wing had also returned safely.

MISSION 19, DECEMBER 19: Flew in top cover flight, while Red and Yellow flights dive bombed in a return mission to the area southeast of Duren. Encountered moderate heavy flak and concentrated light flak. Visibility at the home airbase was extremely poor. It was late afternoon and a heavy fog covered the area. The mission was fairly long and without auxiliary tanks the P-47's were getting low on fuel. Due to the poor visibility, the planes were slower than usual getting on the ground. Since I was in the last position to land, I orbited the air base while planes landed ahead of me. The darkness increased and visibility decreased to the point where the end of the runway was not visible.

To mark the end of the runway for me, two gasoline fires in steel drums were lit, one on each side of the runway. For some unknown reason, the fire on the left side was positioned over a hundred feet down the runway. To locate the runway, the procedure is to visually draw a line between the two fires and fly perpendicularly exactly between the two fires. However, since one barrel of fire was over a hundred feet down the runway, flying perpendicular to the visualized line between the two fires put me on a course about thirty degrees to the right of the runway. As I made my approach with flaps and landing gear down, I was "feeling" for the ground and ready to touch down, when right under my wing I saw four planes of the alert flight that were normally parked just off the end of the runway! I gave the big radial engine full throttle and the fourteen-foot propeller picked me up, and my plane gained airspeed after nearly crashing into the alert flight aircraft. The officer on duty in the control tower suggested that I fly to an alternate air base at Charleroi, about twenty miles farther west. I had no idea where the airstrip was at Charleroi and visibility may not have been a bit better there. As I circled for another approach, I told the control tower operator that my fuel light, indicating twenty minutes of fuel remaining, had been on for fifteen minutes. Besides, I recognized the visual error created by the staggered gasoline drum fires. My second attempt at landing was successful as I mentally noted the runway location in relation to the fires. One normally does not expect the landing at home base to be more hazardous than the mission itself. The goof-up in not placing the steel drums exactly opposite from each other nearly caused a serious accident. With a sigh of relief I expressed my thanks to the Lord for a safe return from the day's mission. Darkness had fallen and the dense fog had settled over the region.

MISSION 20, DECEMBER 24: The dense fog that made landing so risky five days ago continued to cover a vast region and not only kept our planes grounded, but it also provided a cover for Germany's last great offensive on the Western Front, which was eventually called the Battle of the Bulge. After five days, we had a break in the fog and we flew our first mission carrying two 500 lb. bombs and a 200 lb. fragmentary bomb, and dive bombed enemy positions where they had broken through our defenses.

It was Christmas Eve and the situation was tense as our latest information placed the advancing German forces only twenty miles from our airstrip. We were told to be on alert for German paratroopers, and plans were made to fly the P-47's from our airstrip to a landing strip farther west from the front lines. All pilots drew straws to see who would fly the planes out and who would evacuate by truck. Pilots drawing the short straws would fly the planes. I drew a long straw, but ended up with a short straw because several of the pilots had been celebrating earlier in the evening and might have been at risk flying the P-47's at night to a strange airstrip. It was one of the times I volunteered to take over for one of my friends to keep him from endangering his life.

About ten o'clock at night we heard small arms fire at the far end of the runway where a fire was blazing. Someone assumed that the fire was a marker for German paratroopers landings. Pilots are not very well trained in ground warfare, but we all had our carbines ready to defend our positions as all of the P-47 aircraft were still on the ground. As it turned out, the fire was in a GI tent that had caught fire from an overheated stove, and the gunfire we heard was exploding ammunition that was stored in the tent. Everyone was very much on edge after the paratrooper scare and we continued to make plans to evacuate. Just before midnight, information was received that the American troops were holding the line and we were not in immediate danger of being overrun. All evacuation plans were canceled and we were told to return to our chateau and try to get a few hours of sleep so we would be ready for the early morning mission. It was a Christmas Eve I'll never forget.

MISSION 21, DECEMBER 25-CHRISTMAS DAY: We bombed trucks and strafed military vehicles near St. Vith in the breakthrough sector. After my dive bomb run, I spotted a German armored half-track vehicle about two hundred yards from a wooded area. Evidently the half-track had run out of fuel or had broken down and was unable to reach the cover of the wooded area. As I made a strafing run on the half-track, I was greeted by 20mm gunfire from the vehicle. Alerted by the unexpected antiaircraft fire, I made a wide orbit and made my second strafing pass at a much higher speed. I could see the API (armor piercing incendiary) bullets from my eight 50 cal. machine guns striking the half-track, but I could not set it on fire, so I figured the vehicle was out of fuel and would not burn. My second strafing pass, however, did not discourage the two gunners in the vehicle as they continued to fire at me on my strafing run. Once again I made a wide orbit for my third strafing pass with the intention of disabling the vehicle permanently. During a strafing run the gunners in the vehicle were looking straight into the barrels of my machine guns and I was flying into the barrel of the 20mm machine gun mounted on the half-track. As I zoomed by into my orbit, in preparation for another strafing pass, I saw one of the German gunners jump out of the half-track and start running for the shelter of a farmhouse about a hundred yards from the vehicle. The German soldier had seen the wide orbit I made between strafing runs and calculated that he would have time to reach the safety of the farmhouse before I came around again. At the sight of the running German soldier, I instinctively banked my P-47 into a tight turn and was in position to strafe him while he was only half-way to the farmhouse. As my P-47 came roaring down on the soldier, through the gun sight I could see the frightened look on his face. As I leaned forward in the cockpit, I curled my finger around the gun trigger that would unleash a devastating hail of bullets from eight machine guns. In a matter of seconds the enemy would be blown to bits. For whatever reason, I didn't fire my guns. At nearly four hundred miles per hour I roared by the running soldier, passing just a few feet over the top of his head. To this day I'm not certain why I didn't fire my guns at the running German. He was spared from certain death by more than luck on that day.

In the meantime, the remaining gunner in the half-track continued firing during my strafing run. At the start of my next strafing pass, the 20mm tracers once again reached for the P-47, and in return, I fired an extra long burst at the enemy half-track. On the fifth and last strafing run, I drew no fire from the half-track. I reasoned that the gunner had either decided to duck behind the armor plate protection around the gun or my previous strafing run had disabled him. Unable to set the half-track on fire, I left the area to rejoin my squadron members.

MISSION 22, DECEMBER 26: On this mission the squadron leader was looking for targets of opportunity. The target was a convoy of trucks stopped in a town. As we dive bombed and strafed the convoy we encountered accurate, heavy flak. I could see a grapefruit size hole in my left wing. As is always the case, I wondered how much unseen damage had been done to my aircraft. I had no time to continue wondering as our mission controller was directing the squadron toward bandits (enemy aircraft) reportedly in the area. No bandits were encountered and after a short search we returned to base. Upon landing, my crew chief discovered a second hole on the underside of my P-47. I was thankful the flak hits had not caused disabling damage to my plane.

MISSION 23, DECEMBER 27: Flew a close support mission south of Duren, where we dive bombed gun positions with good results. Sighted an ME 262 (German jet powered aircraft) heading back to Germany. Also observed U.S. heavy bombers bombing the town of Euskirchen with devastating results.

Flight of four P-47's preparing to land.

Some landings are rougher than others.

Armed and on the way to the front.

From left to right: Lowell D. Scales, Earl Stenejhem, Don St. Claire, Al "Pop" Zlaten, and Tom McCaffery. (1944)

Missions Flown In 1945

MISSION 24, JANUARY 01: This was an early morning mission dive bombing wooded areas in the breakthrough sector. The German offensive was stopped and Allied fighter-bombers were taking a heavy toll on the stalled German forces. While we were over Germany, the Luftwaffe was making a last ditch stand to neutralize the Allied tactical air power. This operation was named Bodenplatte (base plate) and involved 900 fighters simultaneously attacking Allied air bases. In the time span of a few minutes the raid damaged eighteen Allied airfields and destroyed 300 to 400 Allied planes, besides causing numerous casualties. The losses of the German Luftwaffe were equally severe. An interesting sidelight to the operation is the fact that several German pilots, who were shot down, carried maps clearly marked with a flight course to our airfield. However, because the attack was made at such a low level, navigational errors occurred and other airfields suffered the blows meant for the 373rd Fighter Group. The purpose of the Luftwaffe operation was to cripple the effectiveness of Allied fighter bombers. The operation was successful, but heavy losses suffered during the air raid caused irreparable damage to the Luftwaffe. On the other hand, Allied forces quickly replaced the lost pilots and destroyed aircraft.

MISSION 25, JANUARY 5: Grounded by bad weather for three days, once again we were flying into the breakthrough area. However, this mission was unique in that our flight of four P-47's was assigned to escort a single B-24 bomber flying at 25,000 feet above the "Bulge" battle ground. The mission of the B-24 was to jam the German radio transmissions and we were to protect the B-24 bomber.

This turned out to be almost a four hour mission; my longest.

After being relieved from escorting the B-24, we were vectored towards enemy aircraft near the town of Houffalize. No enemy aircraft were encountered, but several thousand feet below us a squadron of B-24 bombers was on a bomb run over the town. I watched with apprehension as they flew through heavy flak at an unusually low altitude. My concern was not without reason, as I saw one of the B-24s break out in flames and gradually fall from formation. While flying my own aircraft and taking evasive action against the flak coming up at our flight, I could not continuously watch the stricken bomber, but at no time did I see anyone parachute from the plane. The low level bombing mission by the B-24s undoubtedly produced accurate bombing results, but the effort was costly as other B-24s suffered hits from the accurate flak thrown up by German defenders.

MISSION 26, JANUARY 16: Bad weather had kept us on the ground for ten days. Today we dive bombed a railroad yard near Scheleiden, encountering lots of heavy and light flak.

MISSION 27, JANUARY 20: Dive bombed a train west of Euskirchen. Moderately heavy flak encountered.

MISSION 28, JANUARY 21: Dive bombed and strafed an oil train east of the Rhine River. Left the train burning and destroyed buildings next to the track. No mention of flak.

MISSION 29, JANUARY 22: This was an afternoon mission. In the morning I led the alert flight on patrol in proximity to our airfield. Patrol flights were instigated following the Lufftwaffe's surprise attack of January 01.

The afternoon mission was a memorable one for me. The target was the railroad yards at Neuss. The city of Neuss, just north of Cologne, was an important railroad junction that was vital to the German war effort. The veteran Kelly (we had two Kelly's) was leading the mission and as we progressed toward the target, the flak became more intense. I noticed that during our flak evasion we had climbed to 17,000 feet, about one mile above the usual altitude of 12,000 feet, from which we started our dive bomb run. I was leading the last element of two planes scheduled to dive bomb. As we made a wide orbit in the target area, I noticed a lone plane approaching my wing man from the rear. I didn't recognize the plane as being friendly, so I turned to meet the oncoming plane, head on. As soon as I made my turn, the oncoming plane veered off. My wing man was alerted to the strange aircraft behind us, but his job was to cover me and my job was to cover him. As we approached the target, the lone plane once again started closing in on my wing man and again I turned to meet the plane head on and again the plane veered off. Whoever was flying the plane finally got the idea that his company was not welcome. Later the idea was offered that the lone plane might have been a photo reconnaissance aircraft waiting to take photos of the results of our dive bombing; nevertheless, the pilot's actions were threatening.

After the encounter with the lone plane, it was time for my dive bomb run on the railroad yards, and I lost track of the fact I was starting the dive from 17,000 feet. I went into a power on near vertical dive (for more accuracy) and took several seconds longer than usual getting the target centered in my gunsight. I released my bombs and tried to pull my plane out of the dive. The controls were stiff and wouldn't budge! I quickly checked the air speed. Over 500 miles per hour (red line was 500 mph!). I took a quick glance back at the tail to make sure the tail section was not being twisted. A purple haze covered the leading edge of the wings! I realized that I had hit compressibility! Making sure that the needle and ball (one of the flight instruments) were perfectly centered, so as not to put a twist on the tail section, I grabbed the control stick with both hands and pulled back! The controls still didn't budge! As the P-47 plummeted into the denser air, the controls began to ease back and the plane began to pull out of the dive. I pulled back harder as the ground was rushing up at me! The plane responded and the G-forces from the pull out began to cause me to black out! The black out was only momentary and as I pulled up, the speed from the dive lifted the plane to 10,000 feet in what seemed like one big leap. My wing man reported that I had two direct hits on the large railroad station building. I reported to my crew chief that in my dive bomb run I had reached compressibility in his airplane and it should be thoroughly checked for stress damage.

MISSION 30, JANUARY 25: My crew chief had checked over P-47, V5A and found no visible damage from the high speed dive and pull out on my last mission On today's mission we dive bombed and strafed the town of Breklen, north of Linnich. Destroyed buildings, encountered moderate amount of heavy and light flack.

MISSION 31, JANAURY 27: Dive bombed railroad yards near Mayen, west of Koblenz. Also made one strafing pass. Buildings were destroyed, and flak was meager.

MISSION 32, JANUARY 29: Dive bombed and strafed railroad yards northeast of Prum. Destroyed buildings, railroad cars and cut tracks; no mention of flak.

MISSION 33, FEBRUARY 2: Dive bombed railroads southwest of Euskirchen. Encountered accurate heavy flak. One of our aircraft did not return.

MISSION 34, FEBRUARY 3: The target area was completely overcast. We were vectored over Euskirchen and on the mission controller's signal, our bombs were dropped. Bombing by radar was always disturbing to me, since no target was ever visible, and I visualized the bombs dropping on non-military targets and civilians.

MISSION 35, FEBRUARY 4: This mission was another close support mission, but no details were recorded.

MISSION 36, FEBRUARY 6: This proved to be my most memorable mission..........

CHAPTER SEVEN
Behind Enemy Lines

Tuesday, February 6, 1945 started out in the usual manner with a 5:00 a.m. shake on the shoulder accompanied by the Sergeant's familiar "Lieutenant, briefing in five minutes". Truly briefing was in five minutes and since I didn't set my alarm for an earlier arousal, there was not enough time to eat breakfast before the briefing for the morning mission. Directly after briefing those of us scheduled to fly the morning mission were transported the several kilometers to the airstrip being used by the 373rd Fighter-Bomber Group. The weather was typically European winter; snow covered most of the ground, the temperature was below freezing and the low clouds (it's almost second nature for pilots to be acutely aware of the clouds and their movement) were only a few hundred feet above the ground, and were rapidly moving across the airstrip. The thought of the missed breakfast was troublesome, but not overly so, as I knew from the briefing session that the mission was in an area west of the Rhine River and we would be back at our airstrip within about two hours. By air, via our P-47 Thunderbolts, the front lines were less than five minutes away after take off. This morning's mission was to be carried out by the normal squadron strength of three flights of four P-47's per flight. I was assigned to lead the 2nd element of two planes in Red (the lead) flight, thereby assigned position Red 3. We picked up our parachutes and climbed into the cockpit of our normally assigned aircraft (V5A for me) and made the regular routine check of the instruments and fuel gauges. Having done so, we were ready to start the big R2800 Pratt and Whitney radial engines and taxi to the runway. But there was no signal to start engines. After a half hour or more, information was received that the target area was covered by clouds. However, we were told to stay ready for take off on short notice. After over three hours of sitting in the cockpit of the P-47's, Red leader was starting up and began moving towards the runway for take off. Here it was mid-morning and I had envisioned being back from the mission and making up for the missed breakfast by eating a few donuts at the Red Cross donut shack located at the airstrip. The clouds over our airstrip were just as numerous and low as earlier in the morning, but we were informed that the clouds were breaking up over the target area approximately 80 miles to the east. One by one we took off and joined in squadron formation. Loaded down with a full load of 50 caliber ammunition for the P-47's eight machine guns and a 500 pound bomb under each wing, the squadron climbed steadily and purposefully. It was prudent to reach an altitude of 12,000 feet before we crossed the front lines and entered over enemy held territory. Small caliber (light flak) antiaircraft weapons were not effective at that altitude; however, at lower altitudes not only were the small caliber weapons dangerous, but the dreaded German 88's were also extremely accurate. We crossed the front lines at 12,000 feet and received the usual greeting from the enemy antiaircraft batteries and over the radio someone calls out "Flak 6 o'clock level". For some reason not fully established, the first flak bursts were nearly always slightly behind our formation of fighter bombers. However, the black bursts of flak were almost always at the exact altitude we were flying. Obviously the German radar was accurate in determining aircraft altitude. A few seconds after the initial flak bursts, the squadron leader changed course by at least 30 degrees and the entire squadron formation executed the change. As we learned to expect, the next group of flak bursts exploded right on the flight path we had just left. If the flak continues as the squadron penetrates enemy territory, this cat and mouse game of changing flight courses with variations in flight speed and altitude continues, but the general progress of the squadron of P-47's is towards the assigned target area. So much for the routine part of the mission; although getting shot at never was boring or routine.

The heavy cloud cover was breaking up and dark splotches of terrain could be seen below. Looking through the holes in the clouds, from my position as leader of the second element in the lead flight, I suddenly caught sight of a truck convoy moving through the mountainous terrain below. I informed the squadron leader of the convoy but he said he had not seen it through the fleeting holes in the clouds. "Red-3 check it out and make sure it's not one of ours", was the command I received in my earphones. "Roger, Red 4 follow me down", I called to my wing man. I dove my P-47 through a hole in the clouds to get a closer look at the truck convoy to determine if they were enemy or friendly. I pulled out of my dive convinced they were Germans. As I pulled back up to altitude I met my wing man who merely orbited the area and made no move to follow me down to check out the convoy. One can't be too critical of an inexperienced wing man who didn't wish to get too close to the enemy. Red leader still had not sighted the convoy so he said "Red 3, lead the attack". I acknowledged the command and proceeded to make a dive bombing run on the convoy through the hole in the clouds. Usually the dive bombing run was a vertical or near vertical dive that reached speeds that often exceeded 500 miles per hour. I was well on the way down with the convoy in my gun sight, which doubled as a bombsight. Suddenly the lower layer of clouds moved across the opening in the multi-layered clouds, and obscured the ground below from sight.

Immediately I pulled the throttle back to slow the P-47 that was by now plunging earthward in an accelerating dive. I broke through the cloud layer, the convoy was in my bombsight, I dropped the bombs and shoved the throttle forward to gain the speed that I would have had if I had not been forced to throttle back. I was low and slower than usual and felt very vulnerable. Seconds later, 40 millimeter anti-aircraft bursts filled the air around me and I felt the Thunderbolt shudder from stem to stern and I knew I had been hit! Almost immediately, hot engine oil came through the instrument panel and soaked my flight jacket. Another thud and I was hit again! The enemy soldiers manning the antiaircraft guns were determined to destroy the Thunderbolt and pilot who had just bombed their motor convoy. Oil sprayed over the cockpit canopy and I could no longer see ahead! I opened the canopy and was startled to see an evergreen tree whiz by my left wing tip! I had missed death by a few feet! Equally shocking was the sight of flames leaping alongside the left side of the cockpit! Engine oil and fuel continued spraying into the cockpit and the front of my B-10 jacket was covered. If the flames came inside the cockpit I could be aflame in seconds! I called Red leader and told him my plane was on fire! Our control tower personnel, back at the home field, keeping track of our squadron flight over enemy territory, cut in on the radio transmission and said, “Red 3, steer 270 degrees, you’re 30 miles in”, meaning I was 30 miles behind enemy lines and needed to fly due west. The powerful Thunderbolt engine was losing oil rapidly and in a few seconds it seized up internally and the four-bladed propeller came to an abrupt stop. Quickly I feathered the propeller (turned the thin edge of the blades into the wind) to reduce drag and help conserve my rapidly diminishing altitude and speed. I methodically locked the shoulder straps attached to my safety belt to keep from being thrown forward during rapid deceleration during the crash landing that was only a few seconds away. Neglecting to lock the shoulder belts usually resulted in one's face being smashed against the gun sight mounted directly in front of the pilot. I made a quick visual survey of the terrain around me. There was a long, gentle valley to the left which had a railroad running through it and along the railroad track I saw a large group of German soldiers. Ahead of me was mountainous terrain with a sharp cliff straight ahead. My immediate thought was to go straight ahead and try to clear the cliff and crash land on top. I had no desire to land near the German soldiers, who, having suffered under P-47 attacks, had no love for fighter-bomber pilots. I checked my airspeed indicator because I wanted to glide as far as I could using the altitude I still had. Without power, a P-47 glides a little better than a rock. The airspeed indicator was on zero! Undoubtedly, flak from the antiaircraft fire had damaged the instrument or the air tube which activates the gauge. Flames were still leaping past the left side of the cockpit. Bail out! The burning plane could explode at any second, or the flames could enter the cockpit and set my oil and fuel soaked clothing on fire! I still had time! I dismissed the thought of bailing out from my mind because I had not considered parachuting out as a possible option as long as the P-47 was still in a controllable glide. It was common knowledge that at this stage of the war, there had reportedly been an increasing number of pilots and air crew who had been shot in their parachutes before they hit the ground. To crash land on the smooth terrain in the valley, amidst the German troops, would have been simpler, but I had other ideas. "If you want me, you'll have to come and get me", I said to myself. I kept the flaming fighter plane on course toward the cliff ahead, not knowing for certain that I could clear the cliff and not knowing what kind of terrain I would find behind the cliff itself. A falling Thunderbolt doesn't keep you in suspense very long. I cleared the cliff by about 20 feet and made a wheels up belly landing onto the only flat, clear spot in the entire area that just happened (?) to be there. I was amazed that the P-47 was able to glide such a long distance without power. I remember quite clearly wondering if I had enough altitude to reach the spot I hastily selected. The skidding plane quickly came to a stop and I urgently needed to get out, as the flames continued to flare up along the left side of the cockpit. Without delay, I released the safety belt and shoulder straps and attempted to move towards the right side of the cockpit for a quick exit, but something was holding me down! I admonished myself: "Don't panic, look down, see what's holding you". Immediately I saw the problem and detached the oxygen hose clamp attached to my parachute strap and the radio wire attached to my helmet earphones. Released from these restraints, it took but a second to get out onto the right wing and down to the ground. My brain was operating at a rapid pace as the adrenaline flowed. Shot down! One doesn't really believe it will happen! It's always the other guy that gets shot down. But this is for real!

There were large patches of snow on the ground left over from the recent storm. Which way shall I go? I quickly pulled out the tiny compass I carried in my flight jacket (I had another compass in the escape kit in the inside pocket of my jacket) to determine which direction was west. Westward towards the front lines was my ultimate goal. But first, let's throw the Germans off the trail. I deliberately walked through the patches of snow, leaving an easily seen trail of footsteps heading north. I also dropped my parachute along the way. After leaving a trail of about one hundred yards in length, I back-tracked to the crashed airplane, avoiding the patches of snow so that I left no easily visible footprints. One more last look at the burning Thunderbolt and I headed west toward a deep ravine which separated the small flat area, where I crash landed, from the rest of the surrounding mountainous area. This was not the type of mountainous area that I knew back in Colorado where I grew up. But thankfully it was rough enough. I moved quickly, for I knew the Germans would be arriving before very long. I didn't have long to wait! Here they come, two troopers riding motorcycles! By now I was crawling on my stomach, trying to keep my body below the low brush and grass in the area. The false trail worked. They took off in a northerly direction with a roar. This gave me time to crawl to the ravine and cross over to the other side where I continued to crawl as fast as I could without revealing my position. In a short time the two motorcycle troopers were back to the burning plane, probably a bit upset that they followed a trail that led nowhere. After a few minutes, several foot soldiers arrived on the scene, but they only observed the burning aircraft without joining the search. After a quick look around, the cycle mounted soldiers began circling the aircraft in ever-widening circles in an effort to pick up my trail. The flat area where I landed was rather small, and after making two or three ever-widening circles, they reached the ravine I had just crossed. After looking at the steep sides of the ravine for a minute or two they decided it was too steep to cross safely on a motorcycle. Fortunately motorcycle troops don't like to walk and these two Germans were no exception. They turned around and gunned their bikes in the direction from which they came, and the foot soldiers followed after the cycle mounted soldiers. I waited a few minutes to see if they would suddenly return to the area to see if they had tricked me into revealing my cover. They never returned and I headed west at a very fast walk, keeping a sharp watch out for other enemy soldiers in the area. In a few minutes I arrived at a small stream. I anticipated that the Germans might be back with dogs that would be able to pick up my trail. If this were so, I better leave another false trail, so I walked down stream for a considerable distance, then stepped into the stream and waded upstream several hundred yards beyond the point where I first encountered the creek. I figured that by walking in the water I would leave no scent for dogs to pick up. Whether this precaution was necessary or not I don't really know, but I felt I should use every evasive tactic I could. After walking about one half mile in the water I crossed the creek onto the opposite bank and by late that afternoon I had traveled a couple of miles upstream. At this point I was forced to take cover and stay hidden because I sighted several German soldiers cutting firewood in the forest ahead of me. Fortunately my shoes had dried as I walked and my feet were not very cold - yet. Now daylight was ending and darkness was rapidly taking over, hastened by an overcast sky. I was about to spend my first night behind enemy lines. The parachute I dropped near the crash site would have been a welcome cover during the long winter night, but it would have been difficult to crawl while dragging a chute. My empty stomach reminded me of the breakfast I missed that morning. All of a sudden a realization of the gravity of my situation began to settle upon me like a heavy weight. During this period of time when I wasn't actively moving, the shock of what had occurred began to take hold. I was determined not to panic and make any hasty moves. This determination and my belief in the value of prayer slowly began to dispel the feeling of panic. After several hours, the feeling of panic subsided, and I was able to sleep in short duration cat naps. At each awakening period I would remove my shoes and massage my feet to restore circulation and prevent frostbite in the below freezing temperatures. The numerous waking periods provided ample time for prayers. I'm sure my prayers were not unique; I thanked God for getting me safely on the ground in one piece, and requested safe passage out of my situation, and guidance to make the right decisions and movements to reach friendly territory.

It was a long cold night and morning was slow in arriving. The light of day came, but there was no sunshine and there was very little warming. I was anxious to resume my journey toward the front lines. My anxiousness had to be curbed as I spotted several small groups of German soldiers in and around the forested areas where I was hidden. Their activity was unhurried and they were not concerned about concealing their movements. That made sense. They were in a rear area far enough behind the front lines to be secure from observation by Allied troops. Due to the overcast sky, no Allied aircraft would be flying in the area, so they were safe from attack from the air.

The night had been long and now the day was passing slowly, and any plans I had about moving towards the front lines had to be placed on hold. During this time of forced immobility I found plenty of time to ponder my situation and to continue to pray. After more than twenty-four hours, during which I had moved only a few yards, I decided that at dusk I would make my move from my hiding place. It seemed as though dusk would never come, and finally, just before dark, I moved through the forested area and started walking on a compass heading that would take me to the Western Front. I was careful to stay within the fringe of the forest. Darkness fell and after several hours of walking, I came to the edge of the forested area. Ahead of me was a wide open space with small patches of wooded areas. I decided to spend the remainder of my second night in the concealment of the forest. My progress had been slow.

I spent all of the third day hiding in the forest. It became obvious that I would eventually have to leave the cover of the forest and travel across large open areas. Dusk of a winter day arrives suddenly and with it visibility decreases rapidly. With this in mind, I began moving westward, keeping in the fringe of patches of wooded areas as much as possible. Finally I had to walk out of a patch of trees and had traveled about a hundred yards when I heard the noise of rattling pots and pans coming from the other side of a small knoll to my left. Such noises are created only by a field kitchen and dusk was meal time for the German soldiers in the area. I flattened my body into a small depression and looked to see if I could spot any movement of troops heading for the field kitchen. At that moment a German officer stepped out of a patch of trees directly behind me and walked toward the spot where I lay! He kept coming in a straight line on a course that caused him to pass within a few feet of me. I flattened myself closer to the ground and clutched my 45 caliber automatic. However, I felt that any kind of gunfire would alert the enemy troops in the area, and my situation would worsen immeasurably if a German officer were found shot in the area. Fortunately for both of us, the young German officer was pre-occupied. He was whistling a tune and was probably thinking of a Fraulein back home. He passed so close to me I couldn't believe he didn't see me! I continued to lay flat in the depression for I feared that other soldiers would be making their way to the field kitchen for their supper. Dusk quickly turned to darkness and I began to feel confident that I would not be discovered.

Aware of the numerous enemy soldiers in the area, I decided to stay put until later into the night when most of the troops would be asleep. The sky was still overcast, but the clouds had lifted. The night was still very dark and no stars were visible through the high clouds. About ten o'clock I could hear the steady droning of an airplane directly to the west of my location. After several minutes I could tell that it was a night fighter aircraft flying a pattern over enemy territory. The purpose of the flights was to make it more difficult for the enemy to move men and supplies at night. Most of the enemy movement was at night due to the devastating losses created by the Allied fighter bombers during the day.

After the night fighter had droned through several patterns, in what seemed like a routine manner, there was a terrific explosion behind me! A German 88mm antiaircraft battery was firing at the night fighter. Red flashes appeared in the sky as the 88mm shells exploded. The night fighter ceased its steady droning and the engine sound became louder and louder as the plane dived in my direction. When the sound of the plane was almost upon me there were two blinding flashes in front of me and two streaks of fire came right at me! The pilot of the night fighter had spotted the muzzle blasts of the antiaircraft battery behind me, and was retaliating in kind. In the deep darkness of the night, I had no horizon as a visual reference and the two blazing rockets appeared to be heading exactly towards me! I was momentarily terrified! The rockets went over my head and exploded in the area of the German flak battery! I don't know whether the rockets struck the antiaircraft battery or not, but in any case, the pilot returned to flying his pattern in the sky without anymore interference from the enemy. After about an hour the plane disappeared and I figured the enemy troops had settled down. I began to move along, ever westward, toward the front lines. it was after midnight when I decided to stop in a densely wooded area. I estimated that I had traveled about five miles from my last hiding place.

After my experience the evening before, I thought that dusk may not be such a good time to start moving around. It was a good decision, since I noticed that the closer I got to the front lines, the more enemy troop movement I encountered around dusk. However, about five o'clock I scanned the horizon and could see the clouds getting lower and lower. It wasn't long before snowflakes began falling. The wind was calm and I didn't feel overly cold. As a matter of fact, at the moment, I welcomed the snowstorm. Back home I had often waited for an evening snowstorm to go hunting ducks along the creek. Besides, the snowstorm would give me excellent cover as I moved toward the front lines.

I started walking briskly and soon came upon a lone farmhouse. Perhaps it's empty and I could rest there awhile! It was a tempting thought that flashed through my mind. However, caution prevailed and I stayed out of sight and watched the house closely. Daylight was fast turning to darkness and the snowstorm continued unabated. My patient surveillance of the farmhouse proved worthwhile. The back door opened and out came two German soldiers to get firewood. So much for using the farmhouse as shelter. I took out my tiny compass with its luminous dial and headed west as the snowstorm became thicker and wetter. After about two hours of steady walking and periodically checking the compass to make sure I was heading west, I paused. I checked the compass and gave it a shake. The needle remained pointing west. I shook it again. The needle stayed on west. Darn, the compass had gotten wet, causing the needle to stick. It's possible that I had walked in a circle because the snowstorm had cut visibility to only a few feet. In my inner pocket of my flight jacket I had an extra compass. Why did I have an extra compass? I don't know, I just had an extra compass. I took out the dry compass, and by cupping it in the palm of my hand, I could shield it from the snowflakes and keep it dry. Yes indeed, I was very careful to keep the extra compass dry. Bolstered by the knowledge that my direction of travel would be correct, and buoyed by the fact that I had an extra compass, I set out again with renewed vigor. Vigor? It was now nearly four days since my last meal. I had only a couple of high energy caramel squares and a "D" bar in my "escape" kit for nourishment. These items were gone by the second day. Still, I set out with vigor. I came to a graveled road and began to follow the road since it headed west- ward and that's where I wanted to go.

About ten o'clock in the night the snow stopped and there was a dim reflection from the snow that enabled me to see about 100 yards. As I came to a spot where the road was cut through a hill, I could see the outline of the entrance to a small cave in the cut bank. Immediately I thought a cave would be a nice, dry place to spend the rest of the night. I walked up to the entrance and stuck my head inside. I couldn't see anything in the pitch black interior. But I didn't need to see, I could hear the heavy snoring of several people sleeping in the cave. No place for me! I quickly turned to go and physically bumped face-to-face into an enemy soldier! He evidently was coming back into the cave after going out in response to nature's call. He spoke something in German (probably "watch where you're going"). I cleared my throat and muttered under my breath and continued down the road. Good thing it was dark, I thought to myself. That German soldier had no idea whatsoever that he had bumped into an American airman.

I had continued walking on the road for quite awhile, when I began to tire and feel all alone. For the first time since I was shot down I experienced a heavy feeling of discouragement. I prayed and asked God to help me. As I was praying, I felt a warm spiritual presence. I looked around behind me. I even looked up into the overcast sky. I saw no one, but the feeling of someone's presence stayed with me for several minutes and I felt that it had to be Jesus. My feeling of discouragement left me and I gained enough strength to continue on my way. Emotionally I felt more peaceful and relaxed.

After a few more minutes of walking, I began to hear the sound of marching feet. The sound seemed to come from the direction from which I had come. I moved off of the road onto the snow covered field. The sound of marching feet (I'm sure they were not marching in time) came closer and closer through the still night. In the dim light of the reflective snow, I could see a column of German soldiers moving toward the front. Well, they know where the front is, so I'll just walk with them, was the thought I had. My plan was to walk along with them, they on the road and I walking in the field parallel with them. Yet, I didn't want to be seen and on the other hand, I didn't want to be too far away in the field. So I had an idea. I took off my jacket, shirt and winter underwear top. I put my shirt and jacket back on and pulled the white underwear top over my jacket. The generously sized GI winter underwear top covered me nearly to my knees and made a very useful camouflage snow suit. Emboldened by my improvised camouflage, I drew closer to the marching troops and was able to move along with them undetected. Our movement continued in this manner for nearly an hour. It was almost midnight when I saw silhouettes of what appeared to be a large cluster of farm buildings, similar to those I had seen associated with large dairy farms. The column of soldiers stopped at the farm buildings and soon they were all dispersed among the various barns and sheds. This must be it for tonight, I thought. Maybe I could find a small, vacant shed along the outside perimeter of the buildings.

After waiting for nearly an hour for the troops to get bedded down, I began cautiously approaching the farm buildings. I figured my improvised "snow suit" would conceal me on the snow covered ground. I had moved up to within about 100 feet of the buildings, when the still of the night was broken by the persistent barking of a small dog that was barking in my direction! Immediately I laid down in the snow for concealment. The barking of the dog quickly aroused several soldiers who came out to look in the direction the dog was barking. After a couple of minutes of staring at the snow covered field, the German soldiers were convinced the dog was being a nuisance. They picked up the dog and carried it into the barn with them. I agreed, that little dog was a big nuisance. I was convinced that there was no place for me at the dairy farm, so I picked myself up from the snow covered ground and checked my compass for direction. To continue west I had to make a wide circle around the dairy farm. I started walking again with more determination and less vigor than I had earlier in the night. The feeling of loneliness did not return as I circled the dairy farm and intercepted the country road that continued past the farm. I walked for about two hours on the road which continued to head west. Suddenly, I heard the sound of a vehicle approaching from the direction of the front. I looked for a place to hide, but there was no place nearby that would offer any concealment, so I ran out into the open field away from the road where I laid down in the snow and awaited the approaching vehicle. In a short time a truck with a canvas cover, a typical military truck, made its way down the hill, past me and continued on its way. I waited a few minutes to see if there were other vehicles that might be traveling the road. Hearing none, I walked back to the road, checked my compass, and continued on the road which was going steadily uphill. After about an hour, I noticed that the area was becoming more forested. Rather than continue on the road which was becoming more winding, I decided to travel in the forest. As I walked, the night became darker and I could only see a foot or two in front of me. The trees were closer together and I continually ran into branches in my path. To protect my eyes and face, I walked slowly with one arm at eye level to guard my face from the branches. There was no light at all, and the night became pitch black and I was unable to see my path in front of me. I continued to walk slowly but steadily, when suddenly I stopped. I stuck my foot out in front of me and could not feel anything! I backed away from the spot and changed my course so I was moving at right angles to my previous direction. Why had I stopped? I had been walking more or less steadily during the whole night. I was a bit puzzled as to what made me stop and check ahead of me.

I continued walking for several minutes when I decided to stop and wait for the approaching dawn, which was an hour or two away, so that I would have more light to see where I was stepping. Being in a dense forest at night was like being in a closet with the door shut and the light out. When the first faint light of pre-dawn came upon the area, I decided to move ahead and locate a place to conceal myself before daylight. I was in a mountainous type of terrain with a small river (or large creek) on my left and to my right was a road and a pine tree covered ridge beyond the road. In the semi-darkness I made my way across the road and up the slope of the adjoining ridge. The top of the ridge was several hundred feet above the road which followed the stream in the valley. I climbed about two thirds of the way up the ridge where I found a thickly branched evergreen tree that could provide some concealment. I could hear voices, and as the light of dawn unveiled the valley, I could see an antitank gun set up in the road about two hundred feet below me. The muzzle of the gun was pointed down the valley, obviously in the direction of the front lines. How far I was from the front, I was not sure at the time, but I must be getting close! I could see several members of the antitank gun crew moving around the gun emplacement. After closely observing the area below me, I began to scan the valley to see where I had walked during the night. Why had I suddenly stopped in my tracks? There was the answer! Up the valley from me was a two hundred foot high cliff which was directly in the path I was blindly traveling! Why did I stop short of the cliff? Different people have different answers. It wasn't luck. I had been walking steadily most of the night without stopping. Was it the hand of God that stopped me? I didn't feel anything. I now believe it was the Spirit of God instructing my inner spirit to stop. As I mentioned earlier, I prayed continually for a safe journey out of my predicament. Up till now there had been several close calls that could have resulted in death or serious injury. As I lay under the friendly low lying branches of the evergreen tree, I was thankful to be in one piece. Hungry? Yes, but thankful. There was still one objective in my mind, and that was to reach the front lines. I couldn't be very far from the front at this point!

CHAPTER EIGHT
At The Front

Shortly after Christmas of 1944 following the Battle of the Bulge, the General from Wing Headquarters, in his talk to all of the pilots of my Fighter Group, told us that the big push was coming. Our troops were going to drive all the way to the Rhine River. I had every reason to believe that the German troops would be steadily pulling back to the Rhine River. Consequently, the second part of my plan would be to hide out until our troops pushed the enemy back and "rolled over" me and I would again be in friendly hands. It was a good plan and had worked before for others.

But for now, I was pinned down under my friendly evergreen tree. It was a beautiful pine tree about thirty feet high with thick, low lying branches that touched the ground. Branches touching the ground were rather unusual since nearly all of the trees I had seen in my trek toward the front had the lower branches trimmed off. Nevertheless, I was thankful for the concealment the thick branches provided.

I kept a close watch on the gun crew in the valley. There was very little activity in the general area, although several trucks did enter the valley from the east. The sky was overcast on this, the fifth day since my fateful mission and the weather was obviously unsatisfactory for flying. As always during the day, I listened intently for the familiar sound of fighter bombers flying overhead, however, there was no sound of aircraft in the sky. Only thick, low-lying clouds filled the sky from horizon to horizon. Tomorrow it will clear and the drive to the Rhine River will start up again, I kept telling myself.

Shortly before noon the clouds became darker and it began to rain. Rain in February, that seemed strange. Nevertheless, I was thankful it was not cold enough to snow.

The rain began to melt the snow on the ground and the stream in the valley began to swell with the run-off from the rain and melting snow. About midday, while I was sitting under the evergreen tree, there was an explosion in the top of the tree! At the same time, I felt a blow to the back of my neck! During the morning I had observed occasional rounds of artillery shells bursting in the valley below. I knew it was harassing fire from the American artillery men. However, this time the artillery shell hit the tree that was sheltering me! I slowly reached to feel the back of my neck, expecting to see blood covering my hand! I looked at my hand and there was no blood. I was hit by part of a tree branch that was broken up by the tree burst (artillery striking a tree and exploding was called a "tree burst"). The back of my neck was sore, but I was untouched by the flying shrapnel. Again, I thanked God for protecting me from injury. The rain fell steadily into the afternoon. The thick branches of the evergreen tree, that was my hiding place, shed the water from the rain remarkably well despite suffering the tree burst, and I kept reasonably dry. The rain continued and after about six hours my friendly evergreen tree no longer shed water and the rain leaked through and I was beginning to get wet. About dusk the rain stopped and I began thinking about moving to another place of concealment. A spot where I could at least stand up and perhaps be better able to observe the activity in the area.

I had noticed that the stream made a sharp bend to the right about three hundred yards downstream from where I was hiding. I could not see what was around the bend in the stream because the ridge I was on extended to the point where the stream made the sharp turn. Several feet up slope from where I was hiding there was a foot trail running along the side of the ridge. Dusk was rapidly approaching and despite my reluctance to move around at dusk, I decided to venture from under the evergreen tree. I began moving on the trail in a downstream direction. I had walked several hundred feet when I saw someone up ahead about two hundred feet, looking in my direction! Darkness was beginning to settle in, making it difficult to see clearly. I knew the figure was that of a German soldier, but I was certain he didn't know who I was. In the next instant he shouted something at me and I stepped off the trail and into the surrounding brush and trees.

I waited in the brush a short time, fully expecting someone to approach the area where I was. No one came immediately and I was anxious to get to the bend in the river so I could get "the lay of the land" before it became too dark to see. I moved quickly in the direction of the bend in the stream, being careful to stay off the trail and avoid the open areas where my silhouette might be seen against the skyline. In a short time, I arrived at the place where the rain-swollen stream made the sharp turn to the right. I stood on the right bank of the stream and looked to my right around the bend in the stream. In the dim light of nightfall I could see the steep terrain along the right bank. At the same time I could see the outline of a small village in a small, flat area across the creek. Since I was thoroughly wet by the recent rain, I thought I should wade across the stream and try to find a place to spend the night. It was essential to hurry since darkness was beginning to descend upon the narrow valley. During my high school and college years I had waded across many rivers and creeks while fishing and duck hunting. So it was with a certain amount of confidence that I decided to wade the stream at a point where it was about fifty feet wide. I stepped into the ice cold water and waded out about ten feet when the water became more than waist deep and the swift flowing water of the rain-swollen creek swept me off my feet! Instantly, with all my strength, I began swimming toward the opposite bank. After an anxious moment or so I felt solid ground under my feet and began to walk up the shallow bank of the creek. Just as I stepped out of the creek there was a loud pop in the sky in front of me, and the entire area was brightly illuminated by a parachute flare. Quick as a flash I fell on my face on the muddy ground, but just as quickly I raised my head to try to memorize the lay of the land in front of me. The wide open strip of land paralleling the stream, the large, long building on the other side of the open ground, the village buildings to the right of the long barracks-like building, the house and barns several hundred feet to my right. I was desperately trying to memorize everything I was seeing. The parachute flare hung in the sky for what seemed like a minute, casting its brilliance over the area. What a fortunate coincidence, a flare lighting up the area at that precise moment! I knew it was more than good fortune, and I sincerely thanked the Lord for lighting up my path. The flare had been fired from a mortar on the American side of the front lines. Then it struck me, I had been walking for five days and nights to reach the front lines; now I was within mortar range of the front! If I could just find a safe place to hide out for a few days, until our infantry pushed forward and overran my hiding place, I would soon be back with friends. The flare much too quickly went out and in the semi-darkness I could barely make out the buildings that were so brilliantly illuminated only a moment before. I got on my feet and decided to walk straight ahead. I had gone about fifty feet, when in front of me a dimly visible figure of a man shouted at me. I turned sharply to my right and proceeded downstream toward a group of barns I had seen while the parachute flare hung over the area. The shout and my deliberate change of direction was again a most "fortunate occurrence" as I would find out at daybreak.

Very cautiously I approached the nearest barn, for every shelter I had sought the last several days had been occupied by enemy troops. As I slowly approached the barn, darkness began to take over. I stopped about seventy-five feet from the barn and laid on the ground. I wasn't going to barge into a squad of German soldiers bedding down for the night. I observed the area for nearly three hours without moving. The cold I was feeling from my wet clothes and the falling temperature was enough to make me anxious to find some type of shelter for the remainder of the night. I walked up to the first barn, which was an open structure with no door, but would be some protection from the weather. Well, I thought, if I'm this close to the front, maybe I should try to get a bit closer. Obviously a pilot doesn't know very much about what conditions are like at the front. Nevertheless, I moved forward until I came to a rock wall that was higher than my head. Very cautiously I climbed upon the wall until I could see that it was an abutment of a bridge crossing the river I had just swum across. Being cautious and unhurried, I waited. Suddenly there was a low whistle to my left and an answering whistle came from directly below me on the other side of the rock wall. I could see the shadowy figure of an enemy soldier on a bicycle approaching a sentry stationed just below me. The whistle was a password that allowed the approaching soldier to cross the bridge. I wondered, could I duplicate the whistle? Maybe, but what would I run into on the other side of the bridge? I convinced myself that I was close enough to the front and it would be better to hide until morning when I could observe the situation in daylight. I silently backed off from the rock wall. About 75 feet from the wall, I found a small enclosed shed about ten feet square with a door on one side. I carefully entered the shed and found several boxes covered with burlap. I discovered, after some looking and feeling around in the dark, that they were beehives, and I could hear the bees buzzing around inside. I hoped the bees were shut up inside and couldn't get out. Or, if they got out, it would be too cold for them to be very active. The bees settled down inside their hives and I decided to stretch out on the burlap bags covering the hives. I intended to take only a short, cat nap as I had been doing every night. By taking short naps I was able to move around between naps and to rub my hands and feet to keep up circulation and prevent frostbite. Due to lack of food, walking a long distance and exposure to the cold weather, my stamina had reached a low ebb. At any rate, I slept without waking for several hours.

A deafening explosion and flying lumber abruptly awakened me from sleep! A mortar or artillery shell, from our side of the front lines, had landed right next to the shed. The walls and roof of the shed were completely blown away except for one corner two-by-four which was still standing upright. There I was, sitting on top of the beehives, completely out in the open. I thanked the Lord that I was miraculously untouched by the shrapnel and flying debris. Then a humorous thought entered my head and I said to myself, "This is not a very good place to hide". Retaining a sense of humor, even in threatening circumstances, somehow tends to calm the nerves. As I got off the beehives and stood up, I felt a strange tingling in my feet and hands. For the moment my spirits sagged as I realized, that while I was sound asleep, my hands and feet were severely frostbitten. My leather aviator's helmet had protected my ears from the freezing temperatures. Despite my dejected feelings, the situation at hand required some quick action; I needed a place to hide! I went back to the barn I had walked past and waited inside for daybreak. The weather was still cloudy and daylight came slowly over the area on this, the sixth day.

From within the barn I could see that I was in a small village. Then, as I looked around, I made a startling discovery that sent chills down my spine. The open space toward which I was walking last evening was posted "Danger Minen". The area was mined! I clearly recalled that I had changed my direction when the dim figure, in the rapidly falling darkness, had shouted at me. I didn't know whether the shout came from a German soldier or whether the dimly visible figure was an angel (yes, I believe in angels). Either way, I know that is was Divine intervention that saved me from being blown up in the mined area. I thanked God I was still alive. In my mind I thought: What an ironic way for an airman to die, by stepping on a land mine. I resolved to limit my movements after dark.

The weather was still overcast and rainy, but I had been behind enemy lines only six days. I was optimistic. The weather would clear and with close air support our ground troops would overrun my position and I would be back with friendly troops in a short time.

The open barn was not a good place to hide, since anyone walking into the barn would see me. The main part of the barn had a dirt floor, however, on one end there was a raised platform about twelve feet wide that extended the width of the barn. Hay and other types of animal feed were usually placed on these platforms to keep them off the dirt floor and away from the animals. However, there was nothing on this platform. The platform was about two and one-half feet above the ground and this two and one-half feet was boarded up except for one hole near the middle. I crawled through the hole under the platform and moved to the corner against the boarded side of the platform.

My position was such that anyone just taking a casual glance through the hole in the side of the platform would not be able to see me in the corner. My hiding spot was dry and musty, but it did provide concealment. As I looked around to see what I could do to make my hiding place more bearable, I saw an American G. I. overcoat on the dirt floor of the barn. I don't know who the original owner of the overcoat was, but I was glad to have it. I shoved the coat under the platform and dragged it to my secluded corner. I was prepared to stay in my hiding place until the Allied troops overran the area. Although I had nothing to eat for six days, except a chocolate "D" bar and a couple of caramel squares from my "escape kit", which I had eaten by the second day, I had not felt any severe hunger pangs after the third day. By tightening my adjustable G. I. belt, I was able to keep my stomach from feeling empty. This procedure was a poor substitute for food, but it seemed to work.

My frostbitten feet had swollen and I was unable to put my boots on after I had taken them off to inspect my feet. I found a piece of broken glass and managed to split the toes of my boots which made it possible to get my boots back on. The severity of the frostbite of my hands and feet had not yet manifested, although there was a continual tingling and aching of the fingers and toes.

I had eaten the freshly fallen snow and had drunk from the small brook I had encountered on my 30 mile trek to the front lines. But now I needed some more water to drink while I awaited my rescue by our troops. In the so-called "escape kit", carried by each pilot flying a mission, there was a plastic bag, with a closure top, to be used for water. The river I had swum the night before was about fifty yards from the barn I was using as a hiding place. Between the barn and the river was open space, and on the other side of the river the terrain sloped up about three hundred feet.

On the slope were two machine gun nests. One machine gun nest was about a fourth of the way up the slope and the other machine gun nest was half way up the slope. Each machine gun was manned by a single enemy soldier. I surveyed this situation for several hours, trying to figure out a way to get some water from the river and not be discovered. The snow had all melted during the rain the day before and the creek was the only source of water I could see.

I could survive without food, but I knew I needed water. I had observed that there were some civilians still remaining in the village as two or three had ventured out on occasion. After my close encounter with the mine field and the German sentry, I was convinced it could be dangerous and possibly fatal to walk around at night in the dark. Since I had observed that there were some civilians in the village, I envisioned that a bold move in daylight might work. My B-10 flight jacket was covered with engine oil and my olive drab trousers were streaked with mud; as a result I hardly looked like an Allied airman. I found an old black hat hanging on a nail in the barn and put it on, thinking it would help disguise my appearance. I walked with a shuffle, which seemed natural for my frost-bitten feet; a movement I thought would help my disguise. I really didn't think that if I were captured, the Germans would accuse me of being a spy just because I added an old black hat to my otherwise regulation uniform.

Thus physically and mentally prepared, I shuffled slowly out of the barn into the open and made my way toward the river. I saw that the two machine gunners were watching me every shuffling step of the way. There were tense moments as I shuffled closer to the river and closer to the Germans crouched behind their machine guns. I reached the creek without a challenge and kneeled down and washed my hands in the cold, mountain stream. With great effort I made my movements appear unhurried. Concealing my plastic bag was difficult, as I filled it with water. Without noticeably glancing at the enemy soldiers, I turned and, unchallenged, slowly shuffled back to the barn. I was surprised that the German soldiers did not think it rather unusual for someone to walk down to the river, fill a plastic bag with water, and shuffle slowly back to the barn with the bag. Was my jacket so covered with oil, and my trousers so covered with mud, that there was no resemblance to a uniform? Did the black hat and slow shuffle add enough to the disguise that there was no suspicion aroused in the machine gunners, as they watched me every step of the way? Maybe it was the unhurried manner in which I moved that assured them I was one of the villagers. After reaching the barn, I felt a noticeable relief of tension; although, I felt there could still be some investigation of my presence near the front lines. My excursion to the river and back took less than fifteen minutes and the tenseness of the situation was immense. I crawled back under the platform into my hiding place where I could relax, or at least try to relax. Now I had water and believed I could last a few more days until the weather cleared and, with the help of air support, the Allied troops would surge ahead. It never occurred to me that a frontal attack might never be made in this particular sector of the front, or I just didn't want to consider the possibility.

As I looked around under the platform with my eyes becoming accustomed to the semi-darkness, I noticed that a discarded Christmas tree had been shoved under the platform. It seemed to me that if I pulled the Christmas tree over to my side of the opening it would help conceal me in my hiding place. I was very careful to obliterate any foot prints or any other signs that would indicate that someone had crawled under the platform. Darkness came and again there had been no Allied aircraft activity this day. The corner under the platform could prove to be my hiding place for several more days.

I wrapped the G I overcoat around my body and prepared for the long night ahead. Never before in my life had the nights seemed so long as the nights behind enemy lines. Although I was able to stay reasonably warm, my frostbitten hands and feet began to be painful enough to permit only short intervals of deep sleep. The space under the platform was small and the air began to feel close. I noticed a small knothole in a board a few inches behind me, and by pushing my nose up to the knothole, I could get a breath of fresh air. Among the things I thanked God for was the breath of fresh air coming through the knothole. I thought, how much for granted we take so many things, like fresh air. I was amazed how grateful one can be for some fresh air, even the small amount that came through a half inch knothole.

The night passed without any extraordinary action, only the occasional exchange of artillery fire punctuated my fitful sleep. The seventh day behind enemy lines dawned bleak and dreary. The weather was disappointingly cloudy, and I spent what seemed like an endless day in my crawl space, hoping and waiting for the weather to clear. However, fair weather was not to be for the seventh day.

After a long night came the dawn of the eighth day behind enemy lines and there was little promise for the weather to improve. During the early morning hours, I heard the sound of a cow softly mooing in the building next to the barn in which I was hiding. To someone raised on a farm, as I was, that soft mooing sound meant that the cow had a young calf nearby. If the cow had a calf, there was an excellent chance the cow could be a source of milk. Milking the cow would be no problem; milking was one of my chores on the family farm. Obviously it would be too risky to leave my hiding place and try to locate the cow during daylight hours. Cheered by the thought of obtaining fresh milk, I decided I could patiently wait until dark.

I had not seen or heard much activity the last two days. However, the machine gunners were still at their machine guns on the slope across the creek and were easily visible from the doorway of the barn which provided my concealment. I spent a great deal of time hiding under the wooden platform in the barn, but occasionally, when I felt the cramped quarters were too confining, I would crawl out into the open space of the barn to stretch for a few minutes. A dull feeling of hunger in my stomach remained constant. During one of my prayers to the Lord, I thought how good a pork chop would taste. Pork chops were one of my favorite foods.

Near one corner of the barn was an empty fifty gallon steel drum standing on end. I had crawled out to stretch my legs for awhile and as I was getting ready to crawl back into my hiding place, I noticed something on top of the fifty gallon drum. Staying out of the sight of the machine gunners, I cautiously made my way to the drum. I saw that there was a cooked pork chop lying on top of the empty drum. I picked up the pork chop, held it up to my nose to see if it smelled spoiled. It was thoroughly cooked and it smelled good. I reasoned that I could take a bite, and if it tasted unusual or bitter I could spit it out. I took a small bite and chewed it gingerly and finally decided it would be safe to swallow it. After several bites I decided there was nothing wrong with the pork chop. I thanked God for remembering my favorite food and for providing the pork chop for me. I could think of no other way the pork chop would have been placed on the steel drum. From my hiding place I could see anyone who might enter the barn and no one had entered during the two days I had been hiding in the barn. I was always awake and alert during the day and awake until late at night. I clearly recalled that the top of the steel drum was bare the day before when I looked at it. Truly the pork chop was a gift from God!

Although my frostbitten hands and feet were becoming more painful, my spirits were buoyed by the "pork chop from heaven". I was also encouraged by the thought of fresh milk that I would obtain, after dark, from the cow I had heard in the building next to the barn. I crawled back into the hole under the platform and edged back into the corner where I continued to pray and again thanked God for the pork chop.

About mid-day, two young children, a boy and a girl about four or five years of age, bounded into the barn. After looking around awhile they both came to the hole leading under the platform and peered into the semi-darkness of my hiding place. I lay motionless as I looked through unblinking eyelids at the pair of inquisitive young eyes that were trying to see beyond the Christmas tree. The tree, laying on its side, made it difficult to see into my dark corner. After about ten seconds, that seemed agonizingly longer, they jumped up and ran off. Not knowing whether I had been discovered or not, I thought of moving to another location in the barn, but every other place was more open than where I was. I thought it was most unusual for children to be living right at the front lines, but evidently this was the case in many other areas of the front. I repositioned the Christmas tree so it would provide more concealment for my hiding place. No one came immediately into the barn after the boy and girl left, and I let out a sigh of relief. My relief was premature! Back came the two children and with them came a German officer, a Captain, with his polished boots and long overcoat. The children kneeled down and pointed under the platform. The officer bent down and glanced in the direction they were pointing. The Captain didn't want to kneel in the dirt and get his nice, clean uniform dirty and his quick glance didn't give his eyes time to adjust to the darkness and see what the children had seen. By repositioning the Christmas tree, I had improved my concealment. Why would anyone want to stuff a Christmas tree under the platform? At the moment I didn't have time to wonder why blessings happen. The German Captain convinced the children there was no one under the platform and ushered them out of the barn. However, I was not convinced that he didn't believe them, and the rest of the day I crouched back in my corner, expecting German soldiers to come after me at any moment. However, darkness fell and no soldiers came and no German officer. Most significantly, no sharp-eyed children came to take another look at the stranger they had been told they had not seen.

Darkness came, and day eight passed with no Allied aircraft activity due to unfavorable weather. Although I was discouraged by the absence of fighter bomber activity, I was preparing to find a way into the frame building from which I had heard the motherly mooing of a cow to her calf. Having learned that a great deal of activity by the enemy soldiers occurred at dusk and for an hour or so after dark, I did not plan to leave my hiding place until several hours after dark. I thought this would be prudent, considering my nerves were a bit on edge due to my encounter with the children who saw me and the German Captain who didn't believe them. I told myself that about 10 o'clock at night should be a good time to go milk the cow and obtain some nourishing, fresh milk. At 10:00 sharp I unhesitatingly emptied the water from my escape kit plastic bag and crawled from my hiding place under the platform. I was very anxious to find the cow in the adjoining structure and obtain some fresh milk. The "pork chop from heaven" had been a real treat, but the need for more nourishment to endure the winter cold and preserve my strength was a priority in my mind.

The shed that contained the cow and her calf was a wooden structure attached to the side of the barn that was my hiding place. The large shed was fully enclosed with a door at the far end and an open window at the other end. Attached to the cow's shelter was a wooden building that was used as a dwelling. From my observations in Europe, I noticed that many of the various structures were attached one to another: the shed to the barn, the barn to the house, etc. Fortunately the open window, about a two and a half foot square opening, was next to the barn. All I had to do was duck out of the barn and jump up into the window. Making sure I had my plastic bag, I jumped up to the window sill and quietly pulled myself inside the dark shed. I was barely inside the window when a dog began barking loudly. Oh no! Now what have I gotten into? I crouched up against the wall just below the window I had just entered. Breathless, I waited to see what would happen! The dog continued to bark and after two or three minutes the door at the far end opened. A young boy of about twelve or thirteen years of age entered, followed by his little dog, which had stopped barking. The boy carried an oil lantern which he held up to light the interior of the large shed. The lantern cast a weak light, but it was enough to reveal that in front of me was a gaping hole in the floor about ten feet deep and fifteen feet in diameter! I was resting on a wooden ledge about two feet wide that ran along the wall against which I crouched. The cone-shaped hole was similar to a bomb crater. The timbers and boards that had formerly been the floor of the building had collapsed into the hole and were broken so that most of the jagged ends stuck up out of the crater in a menacing jumble of needle-sharp points. One more step and I would have fallen into the crater and been impaled on the jagged points of the broken timbers and boards! I was emotionally shaken by what I saw and by the thought of what a horrible fate I had just been spared. The fact that this bizarre circumstance was so unexpected caused my nerves to be on the raw edge. This large shed had all four walls and a roof. The presence of a ten-foot deep hole in the middle of an enclosed shed was startling as well as puzzling. The light from the lantern was too dim to see if there were shrapnel marks on the walls or to tell if there was evidence that the roof had been repaired. To this day I'm not certain what caused the crater-like hole in the floor of the shed. Perhaps it was a below-ground cellar that had been collapsed by a mortar or artillery shell. There are many possibilities for the origin of such a crater, but I've had no strong inclination to prove or disprove any assumptions as to how it occurred. Anyway, there it was and there I was.

As the young boy held up the lantern, he looked toward the far corner, at his end of the shed, where the cow and calf were located. The dim light of the lantern did not clearly light up the shadowy end of the shed where I crouched low against the wall. The boy directed his attention to the cow and her calf, which was in a separate pen. The little dog was content to follow its master and seemed unaware of my presence. Having satisfied himself that the cow and her calf were all right, the young boy and his dog left the shed and went back into the adjoining house.

I thanked God for saving my life one more time by His timely intervention. It was highly unlikely that the dog had heard my movements, since I understandably moved with utmost caution. I'm convinced the boy and his dog were used to provide the light I needed to keep me from falling into the deep hole full of sharp, broken timbers and from being severely injured or killed.

Despite the harrowing experience with the crater filled with sharp, broken timber, my determination to obtain milk from the cow, in the other end of the shed, was stronger than ever. The crater was sealed off from the far end of the shed by a board fence that kept the cow and calf from falling into the ten foot deep hole. In my mind I visualized what I had seen in the light provided by the boy's lantern. By staying on the narrow ledge close to the wall, I could make my way to the fenced off area where the cow was kept. I made no move inside the pitch dark shed for quite a while, thinking the boy might return again to check on the cow and calf. At last I made my way carefully along the narrow ledge. I reached the fence that had been constructed around the crater. I don't know how well cows see in the dark; however, either by sight or instinct, the cow knew someone was approaching her and her calf. She began to move around in a restless manner and mooed softly to her calf. I stopped my approach toward the cow so she wouldn't be overly disturbed. In a low voice, I said, "Easy now, easy now". Being a German cow she probably didn't understand English, but my soothing tone seemed to have a quieting effect on her. My approach seemed agonizingly slow, but I had to be cautious. This was important and I couldn't blow this opportunity. I needed her milk. In the back of my mind I was hoping the young boy wouldn't come back to check his cow one more time.

Finally I was close enough to reach out and touch the animal. She didn't flinch and I slowly moved around to the milking end. I could already taste the fresh milk and was beginning to have some feeling of success in this venture. I located the spigots (teats) and began to milk the cow and squirt the milk into the plastic bag. After a very short time of milking the supply of milk stopped, and I had only a large cupful of milk in my plastic bag. I tried all the spigots - there was no more milk. I figured someone had milked the cow in the evening at the normal time, and then allowed the young calf to nurse on what was left. I glanced at my watch. It was only 10:30 p.m. and the cow couldn't have had enough time to manufacture very much milk. Well, I thought, we'll see about this. I'll be back about 3:30 in the morning and I'll be the first in line. I looked at the cupful of milk in my plastic bag and decided I might as well drink it on the spot since I was coming back for more in the morning. To make it last, I drank the fresh, warm milk in small sips. Back home I was never fond of fresh, warm milk, but this was extraordinarily good. I gave "Bossy" (we were on friendly terms now) some extra hay, from a pile outside of her pen, and told her to get on with making milk. I carefully made my way along the ledge to the open window and back to my corner under the platform in the barn.

I was determined to be the first to milk "Bossy" in the morning. Waking up early was no problem, sleeping was the problem. My frostbitten hands and feet were throbbing painfully without stopping. Sleeping was a fitful exercise and the pain in my hands and feet awakened me every few minutes. For the first time I began to wonder how long I would have to hide out until the Yanks pushed the Germans back and I would be back in friendly hands. Every time I was awakened by the pain in my frostbitten hands and feet, which happened sporadically during the night, I checked my watch. At 3:30 in the morning I made my way back into the adjoining shed where the cow and calf were sheltered. I cautiously made my way along the edge of the outside wall, ever aware of the unseen crater just inches away. "Bossy" had eaten the hay I had given her and there was a good supply of milk available. I filled my plastic bag, took a long drink from it, and topped it off before making my way back to my hiding place. This was the ninth day and it started out well. I had milked the cow and successfully made my way back into hiding without being discovered.

I spent most of the ninth day in my hiding place in the barn. Several times I crawled out from my hiding place to look outside in hopes of seeing some signs of improving weather conditions that would bring Allied fighter bombers over the front. The unfavorable weather dampened my hopes for significant activity by our ground forces, since they often waited for air support before starting a drive against the Germans.

Morning of the tenth day revealed another cloudy day that promised no fighter bomber close support activity. I drank sparingly from my supply of cow's milk contained in the plastic bag that held a bit less than a gallon. The milk subdued my hunger pains. However, I was faced with another grave concern. My frostbitten feet began to develop sore spots that I feared might develop into gangrene. As a boy I had read about the difficulty the World War I doughboys had with gangrene.

The prolonged period of bad weather was causing me to lose hope that the Allied forces would start a big push soon. I began to wonder what was in store for me. During the morning hours I drank all the milk I had. Since I was confident that I could milk the cow in the adjacent shed when my supply ran out, I saw no reason to be overly conservative with my milk supply. However, about mid-day I was beginning to get thirsty and in need of a drink of water. I could see the German soldiers still manning their machine guns just across the river less than a hundred yards from me. I didn't feel like risking another trip to the creek in full view of the ever watchful enemy soldiers. There was, however, an alternative. I remembered that a small tributary stream flowed into the river immediately upstream from the bridge I had encountered my first night in this village. If I made my way around the cluster of buildings attached to the barn, in which I was hiding, and stayed on the opposite side from the machine gunners on the slope, I might reach the tributary stream undetected. After observing the immediate area for about an hour, I stepped out of the barn and stayed close to the buildings. By close I mean right next to them, for I had no desire to get out into the posted mine field which was on this side of the buildings. I figured the Germans surely wouldn't place mines right up against the buildings; and then again, they might! I reached the little stream without incident. The rapidly flowing water was clear and cold. Without any additional thought, I knelt down and took a drink and swallowed. Oh, no! I said to myself, as the water left a barnyard taste in my mouth. In all probability the water was contaminated and I swallowed some without first tasting it. But it looked so clear and clean. No sense in quenching my thirst with this water. I made my way back to the barn and my hiding place under the platform. My mistake of drinking from the contaminated stream cast a feeling of discouragement over me and my spirits sank to a new low.

The day, the tenth or was it the eleventh, since I was shot down, I was no longer certain. The day ended with no air activity and the front was relatively quiet. I cat-napped during the night as the pain in my frostbitten hands and feet intensified. About three o'clock in the morning I paid another visit to the friendly cow next door and replenished my supply of milk.

I was awake before daybreak with a sick feeling in my stomach and a strong call to go to the bathroom. Just as

I feared, the water I drank was contaminated and I had contracted diarrhea. At the moment, with all my other inconveniences, I didn't need diarrhea conditions. The severe attacks of diarrhea continued until daybreak.

I decided to remove my boots and socks and examine my feet because they had become more painful. I didn't like to remove my boots because it was difficult to put them back on over my swollen feet. I removed the boots and socks and noticed that the sores on my feet were becoming larger. By now my spirits were sagging and I prayed with more fervor than ever that God would see me through this situation. I thanked Jesus for His presence in spirit and included a bundle of Hail Mary's. Being rescued by friendly troops in a surge of the front lines was becoming only a faint hope. I spent this, the eleventh day, in my hiding place in the barn. Like on other days the weather was discouraging, and there was no air activity on the front lines. During the day and the night following, the consequences from drinking contaminated water became more apparent with time, adding to my discomfort.

I decided to move out from the barn to a location that would provide a better view of the front lines. I ruled out moving at dusk or dark after my near encounter with the mine field. Dawn had not broken yet, and I decided to look around and see what the rest of the village looked like. I had no idea how many enemy soldiers were in the village or where they were billeted or how the front lines ran. All I knew was that I had to move out on this the twelfth day behind enemy lines. I could no longer stay in one place and wait. Taking my plastic bag half full of milk, I moved cautiously along the side of the buildings away from the river and the emplaced machine gunners. I crossed the little stream from which I drank the polluted water. I didn't realize it at the moment, but I would many times over regret the mistake of drinking from that stream. I came to the road that led to the bridge where the sentry was stationed my first night in the village. So far, so good, no one had spotted me. Several low profiled sheds were along the other side of the road. I crossed the road and opened the door to one of the sheds. The dirt floor of the shed was covered with loose straw. The shed was not very large and I moved toward a corner in the back. There was no place of concealment and I sat down in the straw to ponder my next move. I noticed there was a hen's nest in the other corner and there were two eggs in it. I still had my plastic bag half full of milk and I broke the two eggs into the bag of milk and shook the mixture. I figured fresh eggs and milk should provide some nourishment. Ordinarily I preferred my eggs over easy, but I was in no position to be choosy. I drank the egg and milk mixture with some difficulty since I wasn't too keen on the taste of raw eggs. No sooner had I swallowed the eggs and milk when the scourge of diarrhea hit with a vengeance. I had barely recovered from this latest urgency when the door of the shed suddenly opened! A young girl, about twelve or thirteen years of age, stuck her head inside the shed and was startled to see me lying in the straw. With about a two weeks growth of beard, dressed in an aviator's jacket that had seen better days, muddy trousers and boots that had been cut open from tongue to toe, I must have been an unusual sight. Certainly different compared to the neatly dressed German officer I had seen in the barn several days ago. I expected the young girl to drop her egg basket and run screaming to the German soldiers. The young, blond haired, blue eyed child, probably aged beyond her years by the rigors of war, stood her ground and gently spoke in German "Amerikan?" "Wounded?" I nodded my head slowly. Her surprise was understandable, yet she did not appear to be afraid of me. Suddenly she shut the door and left. Well, this is it, I thought. She'll be back, accompanied by German troops. I was in no condition to move out rapidly, and where I would go without being shot by front-line soldiers, who were understandably nervous on the trigger? As I waited for the Germans to come and get me, the door to the shed opened again. It was the young girl and she was alone. She looked at me, stepped inside, and held out her hand. She had a piece of cake in her hand which she wanted me to take. I took the piece of cake and, as our eyes met, I thanked her for it. Then she stepped back and excitedly motioned with both hands for me to go. I could understand her wanting me to make a quick departure. In her compassion she had just given some food to an enemy airman, and she would be dealt with severely if I remained and was later discovered by German soldiers. I nodded my head and she left, shutting the shed door behind her. I thanked the Lord for the young girl's generosity and compassion, and I quickly ate the cake so there would be no evidence of food remaining. I felt reasonably sure the girl would not immediately inform the Germans that an American was in the shed. However, I didn't know how many other people in the house might know of my presence. Besides, I didn't want that young girl to be endangered in any way because of my presence. I needed to move on. By now it was daybreak and quite light outside. I wanted to move to higher ground where I could get a better look at the lay of the land and get a better idea of what the conditions were in the front lines.

CHAPTER NINE
Captured

I got up on wobbly legs and left the shed. I saw no one and proceeded toward a large building that appeared to have been a store at one time. My hastily conceived plan was to go up the next road toward the hill outside the village. I stepped around the corner of the building and came face to face with three German soldiers about fifty feet away! I guess this is it, I thought. I just stood there as one of the Germans fumbled with his holster and drew his pistol, pointed it at me and at the same time signaled for me to raise my hands. I stood perfectly still with my arms at my sides. They quickly surrounded me and searched my jacket and took my 45 caliber automatic that was Air Corps issue to all pilots. Physically I must have looked as bad as I felt, because two of the soldiers left quickly and returned with a stretcher and placed me on it. I learned that I had been captured by Austrians who were medics in the German army. Thank God again for favors, since it was known that some sectors along this particular front were reinforced with S. S. troops. S. S. troops were not known for their kind treatment of captured enemy. My three captors began interrogating me in German, but I shrugged my shoulders, indicating that I didn't understand German. Then one of the soldiers left and returned with a man wearing a Roman collar who, I presumed, was the village priest. The priest began asking questions in English. He especially wanted to know where my comrades were. It took me a while to convince him that I flew alone. Eventually it was established that I was a fighter pilot. Being a captured fighter pilot seemed to be more desirable than being a captured bomber pilot. Fighter pilots did not drop bombs on innocent civilians as did the bomber pilots. I later learned that the

Germans respected their enemy in a certain order. The infantryman, who presumably shot only at other infantrymen, was the most respected. Following the infantryman, the fighter pilot was next in the order of respectability because he fought only against other fighter pilots high in the sky. Anyway, I was somewhat relieved that I was classified as a "Jagdflieger", and not a hated Bomber Flieger.

The village priest gave up on his interrogation and the Austrian medics, serving the German army, carried me on the stretcher to a large shed located at the opposite end of the village from where I had been hiding. Although I had seen only five civilians, the two children who brought the German officer to the barn, the young boy with his little dog, the young girl who gave me the piece of cake and the village priest, I had the feeling there were other civilians in the village. I couldn't imagine trying to live day to day so near the front lines.

about mid afternoon, two German officers arrived at the shed. The men were older, about in their late forties. They were not the arrogant, Nazi-type that I had heard of and was to encounter at a later date. I presumed they were probably reservists who were called up for Hitler's last stand. "Where were you shot down?" they asked in heavily accented English. I pointed to a corner of the shed and said "many kilometers". As I held up my arm and pointed, I noticed that my hand trembled involuntarily. Although physically I wasn't in the best of condition, mentally I was very alert and determined to tell my interrogators nothing of value. "When were you shot down?" "Many days ago," I answered. My unshaven and generally unkempt appearance gave credence to my answer. As the interrogation proceeded, they wanted to know how I had crossed the rivers. When I told them I swam the rivers, they replied

"You swam the Rhine River?" I had a feeling the two officers were not experienced interrogators, and when they started answering their own questions, I was convinced of it. I nodded my head, knowing full well the river I swam was much smaller than the Rhine, but sometimes a person just can't resist telling a lie. Then they asked, "How could you travel so far?" "I walked", I replied. "Where was the German army?" "How could you do this?" "I walked at night and I saw many soldiers." They looked at each other in unbelief. Then they asked a more sensitive question: "Where is your airdrome?" I wasn't about to tell them I flew from an airstrip located in Belgium, only five minutes from the front lines. So I raised my arm again and deliberately caused my hand to tremble more than it did previously. I pointed to the roof of the shed and, trying to sound a bit delirious and incoherent, I said, "Many, many kilometers". "England?" they asked. Here they go again, I thought, answering their own questions. "Ya, ya, England", I replied. I figured it was no secret that there were Allied aircraft in England. "How many planes do you have in England?" was the next question. By now I realized that my faking of a semi-delirious condition was going over rather well. So, raising my shaking hand and arm, I pointed at the roof of the shed and replied, "We have millions, millions of planes". "How many?" they asked. "Millions…millions", was my faked semi-delirious reply. The two German officers looked at each other, shook their heads in frustration and, with a departing glance at me, they left. Inwardly I was smiling; I had gotten through my first interrogation and had given the enemy no information of value. I knew full well that the two German officers who questioned me were amateurs at interrogation. They were in no way representative of the skilled and unrelenting interrogators all Air Corps flyers were told to be on guard against if captured. Mentally I felt good about my successful encounter with my interrogators.

An older man in his early fifties, also an Austrian medic, was placed in charge over me for the night. The shed, which was our shelter for the night, was open at one end, and provided minimal protection from the winter cold. I was given a blanket for cover and laid down on some straw in the corner of the shed with my Austrian guard nearby. In the other end of the shed were two young German soldiers. They taunted me and amused themselves by making sounds of an aircraft motor, then the ack, ack sound of a machine gun, then the sound of a crash, followed by laughter. This scenario was repeated several times, always ending in laughter. Since I made no indication that I noticed their derision, they soon gave up and settled down. They were able to settle down, but I was not able to do so. My frostbitten hands and feet were causing me considerable pain, but most of my discomfort was being caused by continuing diarrhea (which eventually proved to be dysentery, which is more severe and prolonged). During the night my emergency need for the bathroom occurred about every hour. The "bathroom" was a conventional two-holer located about one hundred feet behind the shed which was our shelter. I didn't have the strength to walk to the outdoor toilet on my own and every time nature unnaturally called, the Austrian medic helped me to and from the outhouse. I'm relating the happenings of the night not only to maintain continuity and to describe my physical condition, but to emphasize a significant circumstance. Although I spoke very little German and the Austrian medic, who proved to be my benefactor, spoke little English, we managed a limited conversation. I found out that the medic's wife and daughter had both been killed in an American air raid on Vienna. The thought flashed through my mind: this man's wife and daughter were killed by American airmen, and I'm an American airman, a captive in his charge. Certainly this Austrian medic, whose family had been killed by American bombers, had a right to be bitter against all American fliers. I detected no such bitterness, and the man literally took care of me all night, treating me with compassion. Was it luck that I had this man as my guard for the night? Possibly it was luck. Was it luck that the man's bitterness and distress, at the loss of his wife and daughter, was subdued by his compassion for a very sick enemy airman who was at his mercy? I doubt it. Only divine influence causes compassion to overwhelm bitterness. I thanked God for placing me in the custody of this kindly man who helped me through the night.

The next morning I was loaded on a farm wagon pulled by two horses. I bid farewell to my Austrian medic friend who had helped me through a miserable night. Two other German soldiers became my guards for the journey. The weather was cold and the sky was still overcast. We had traveled until late afternoon when we arrived at what appeared to be a hastily established field hospital in a vacant building. Several wounded German soldiers were lying on the floor in the building. The night was long, but not as miserable as the night before, and I missed my Austrian medic friend.

The next day the wounded German soldiers and I were transported by truck to a hospital at Steinfeld, Germany. This time I was glad the sky was overcast and our unmarked truck would not be in danger of being strafed by Allied aircraft. My severely frostbitten hands and feet pained continuously and my dysentery continued unabated. The German doctors and medics were too busy taking care of the flow of wounded German soldiers to pay any attention to me. I spent my time between my bed and the bathroom.

I was in the hospital at Steinfeld about a week when, along with German soldiers, I was moved by truck to a hospital at Roggendorf, Germany. Again, thankfully, the sky was overcast and there was no danger of being strafed by friendly aircraft. It was a well know fact that fighter bombers pilots strafed anything that moved that was not painted with a red cross. We arrived at Roggendorf an hour or so before dark. The hospital at Roggendorf was strictly make-shift and beds were available only for a few.

I found a spot in the corner of a room where I could lay down. Almost immediately a non-com followed by a medical officer came over to me. The medical officer spoke English and commanded me to follow him into another room which was vacant and had windows opening up to an open courtyard. In stern tones the officer began to interrogate me with the basic starter questions. "What is your unit?" "Where is your unit based?" I replied I could only give him my name, rank and serial number. I had pictured in my mind what a German Nazi looked like and how they acted. This arrogant officer fit the description to a "T". " I will see that you will talk", he snarled. I was aware of the tales and rumors of the ruthless methods German doctors used to obtain information from prisoners. In my imagination I foresaw nothing less than certain torture and maybe even the threat of castration ahead for me. Yet I steeled myself not to give the enemy any useable information. Before the Nazi-like officer could snarl out another threat - all hell broke loose!

Artillery shells exploded in the courtyard and in the surrounding area. The German medical officer disappeared in a hurry and the non-com came and escorted me back to the corner I had previously occupied. Darkness had fallen and still the Allied artillery barrage continued. Either the shelling caused a power failure or the lights were turned off, causing the German medics to scurry around with flashlights and lanterns. Soon a stream of newly wounded German soldiers was being carried on stretchers into the make-shift hospital. The wounded were so numerous that in a short time every spot on the floor was occupied. Since I had already visited the latrine, I knew there was a window leading from the latrine to the open courtyard. If we are being shelled so heavily I figured the Yanks couldn't be very far away and were planning an attack. This was a golden opportunity to escape. In the darkness and in the confusion of the incoming deluge of wounded soldiers, my movements wouldn't be noticed. All I needed to do was to get out of the building and find a place to hide where I could survive the shelling by our artillery. Despite my high fever and severe chills, I was able to make my way to the latrine on unsteady legs. In the latrine I noticed that the open window leading to the courtyard was about five feet above the floor. With all of my remaining strength I pulled myself up to the window sill and then I lost consciousness. I have heard the saying "The spirit is willing but the flesh is weak". When I came to, how much later I don't know, I was lying inside the latrine with two German soldiers standing over me. My spirits sagged and I realized I was physically too weak to escape. The Germans suspected that I had attempted to escape and they carried me back to my corner and took my boots.

I still had three blankets that I was using to keep warm as I was still having severe chills. As additional wounded were carried in, there arose a shortage of blankets and soon my three blankets were reduced to one. I realized it was in my best interest not to complain and I hoped I would be able to keep one blanket. After what seemed like several hours, the shelling ceased and the stream of wounded stopped. I was hoping that the German medical officer, who had started to interrogate me and had threatened to make me talk, was much too busy taking care of wounded and would not bother me during the night. I thanked God for rescuing me from the threatening Nazi, even though I thought calling in an artillery barrage was a bit unusual, but then, we have a most unusual God.

By morning my chills had subsided; although, my dysentery was still taking its toll of my remaining strength. I had eaten nothing for days and only drank water a few times. Before daylight came there was flurry of activity as all the wounded were being loaded onto a train, that had been brought into Roggendorf under cover of darkness. The train was a mixture of box cars with bunks and regular passenger cars. Near the end of the loading, I was given my boots and escorted to the train by a German Sergeant; who half carried me along the way and loaded me into a passenger car with wounded who could walk alone or with help. The weather was overcast and the train arrived safely in Cologne, Germany about daybreak. I did not see any red cross markings on the train and presumed it was being used to move troops to the front; consequently, the train would be open to attack by Allied fighter aircraft. The train remained parked for several hours in what appeared to be a concrete lined tunnel. About mid-morning the train began to move slowly out of the tunnel, but after traveling but a short distance, the train stopped with a jerk and began rapidly moving back into the tunnel. From the excited bits of conversation between the German soldiers, I was able to determine that Allied fighter aircraft were in the immediate area, and the train was moved back into the tunnel to avoid being strafed.

After about an hour the train began to move out of the tunnel and out into the open. Everyone, including me, was concerned about being attacked by Allied aircraft.

The thought of being strafed by friendly aircraft was a bit unnerving because I knew how deadly the fighter bombers were. The cloudy weather, that had kept the Allied air power grounded for so long, was prevailing. Under the cover of the low lying clouds, the train load of wounded moved across the bridge spanning the Rhine River at Cologne. As we crossed the wide river, my hopes of escaping and eventually returning to the Allied side of the lines suffered a severe setback. The trainload of wounded proceeded through the country for several hours before finally stopping at a town called Arnsberg, in the heart of the Rhineland. All of the wounded German soldiers were transported from the train to another hastily set up hospital. I guess all hospitals near the front were hastily set up. A series of two story barracks-like buildings had been converted into a hospital. The complex of buildings had previously been utilized as an officer's training school. I was assigned a bed near the toilet facilities which was most convenient since my dysentery had not subsided. By this time my frostbitten hands and feet were very painful and even the weight of the bed sheets on my feet was painful. I often wished for a cardboard box to place over my feet so the sheet wouldn't touch them, but that was only wishful thinking. The first few days, at this make-shift hospital, were filled with a flurry of activity as the small medical staff worked unceasingly to care for the overwhelming number of casualties distributed throughout the various buildings. The majority of the wounded soldiers were suffering from serious shrapnel wounds. I was thankful that my condition, although painful, was not as severe as the wounded I observed. With typical German efficiency, a semblance of orderly routine was established by the medical staff.

A few days after I arrived at Arnsberg, a young, English-speaking medical student came to me with a

German officer who was the Commandant of the hospital. The young man's name was Kurt and he explained to me that the Commandant had a question for me. Since this recently established hospital compound had been an officer's training school, the roofs of the buildings had no red crosses on them to indicate to Allied airmen that the whole complex of buildings was now a hospital. Whenever buildings marked with red crosses were sighted from the air, we never intentionally bombed such areas. (I've often wondered how many hospitals were hit during night bombing raids and during daylight bombing through the clouds?) The Commandant wanted to know how large the red crosses should be so they could be seen from the air; since I was a pilot, he assumed I should know. We discussed the size of the roofs of the buildings and the size the red crosses should be. The Commandant stated that the sizes I suggested were too large and could smaller crosses be seen. I said the larger sizes are more easily seen, but it seems that the larger size was not the problem. The Commandant, through Kurt's interpretation, explained that a very limited amount of red paint was available. I advised him to paint the building in the center and scatter a few red crosses on buildings around the perimeter of the area and hope they will be seen. The Commandant half-nodded in agreement, but was not too happy when I suggested the roofs of the buildings be painted with crosses without delay. Since Allied Intelligence listed the whole area as an officer's training compound, the area could be bombed at any time.

Before he left with the Commandant, Kurt informed me that I was the only Allied prisoner in the hospital. After a few days, Kurt showed guarded signs of being friendly toward me. I say "guarded signs" because being openly friendly with captured enemy was not the thing to do.

Again I recalled the Austrian medic who lost his wife and daughter during an American air raid. What a blessing he had been to me as he compassionately took care of me during one of the worst nights I had experienced behind enemy lines. Kurt also proved to be a blessing to me. He came to talk with me every day and sometimes twice a day. Mostly we talked about things not related to the war. To me it was good to hear conversation in English, a language I could understand. However, the most interesting part of Kurt's conversation occurred when the two of us were alone. After about three weeks at Arnsberg, I was able to walk around in the hospital ward. Although walking proved to be extremely painful, I was glad to be on my feet once again and felt I needed the exercise.

I was painfully aware of the fact that as soon as I took a drink of water, within the minute I had to go to the latrine with my dysentery. So I decided not to drink water for an extended period of time. My "no water" diet curtailed my dysentery, but I did get dehydrated, so I drank water again with the same unfavorable results. Back to a "no water" diet I went. During one of my walks around the building with Kurt, I saw a half of a loaf of bread on one of the officer's vacant desk. With a quick glance around I saw that no one was watching and I quickly grabbed the bread and hid it under my jacket. I really didn't have any qualms about "liberating" the bread from the enemy. When I got to my bed I concealed the bread under the bedding. During the night when everyone was asleep I would eat part of the dried bread. After three nights the bread was gone and the effects of my dysentery were greatly reduced. The German doctors noted that my trips to the latrine were less frequent and decided to move me to another section of the ward. I was placed in the last bed in the ward next to a small kitchen. In the bed to my left was a German Sergeant who had been wounded by shrapnel from artillery fire. He was semi-ambulatory but spent most of the time in bed. He spoke a little English and tried to converse with me on occasion. He was relating some of his experiences at the front and commented on the superior firepower of the Allied Forces. "We fire one round of artillery and we get five back from the American side." I do not believe this former stalwart in Hitler's army had any false hopes of victory at this stage of the war.

Several nuns, dressed in attire of their order, including the traditional veil, served in the hospital. At the end of the day two or three of the nuns would end up in the small kitchen next to my bed. Their routine ended when they finished washing dishes at the kitchen sink. The nuns had noticed the St. Christopher medal I wore around my neck and were friendly towards me. One evening I offered to help them wash the dishes. They thanked me for my help and as I turned to leave, they beckoned to me and handed me a couple of boiled eggs. I thanked them for the eggs and figured it was from their personal food supply. Before I left for my bed, they admonished me to keep their generosity a secret by placing their fingers over their mouths in the universal "be quiet" gesture. I shook my head indicating that I understood. It wouldn't do at all for anyone to know that they had befriended an enemy airman. I hid the eggs in my bed and about midnight, when everyone was asleep, I peeled and ate the eggs. I hid the eggshell peelings in my shoe and later disposed of them. I remembered to thank the Lord for the treat of the hard boiled eggs. The eggs were a welcome addition to the small portion of food served twice a day. Almost all of the caring of the wounded was done by male medics; however, there was a young, German nurse who visited our ward daily and ended up at my bed, which was the last one in that end of the building. Over a period of time I learned that her name was Elsa. Elsa spoke enough English so that we could have a limited conversation. I also learned that Elsa had been a nurse on the Russian front but had contracted pneumonia and was sent back to Germany to recover. During her visits I found out that Elsa was only twenty-one years old, but in appearance she looked older, beyond her years. I couldn't help but feel sorry for this young nurse. I had noticed that she, probably out of curiosity more than anything else, seemed to spend more time talking with me than she did with the wounded German soldiers. In my own mind I wondered if the German soldiers in my end of the ward noticed that she was extra friendly towards me, an enemy flyer. One day Elsa was talking to me and began to tickle my feet. She said, "You are so serious and never smile". Under normal circumstances it would have been easy to smile at this pretty young nurse. However, I had no intention of even appearing to be friendly with Elsa while the hostile German soldiers observed and listened to our daily conversations. So in answer to her statement, I said, "I will smile when the war is over". I hoped her well-meaning friendship toward me wouldn't arouse any bitter feelings in some German soldier to the extent that my life would be in danger. I thought to myself, after coming this far with the Lord's help, I'd sure hate to "wake up dead" some morning, a victim of some irate German soldier. Elsa continued her daily visits to my end of the ward and I continued to be polite but unsmiling and the German soldiers in my end of the ward continued to observe my reactions to Elsa's visits.

One day Kurt came to me and said the Commandant had told him that if I gave him my word that I would not try to escape, I could go outside with Kurt and walk around the compound. I told Kurt that as an officer I was obligated not to give my word not to escape. Kurt nodded his head as if he understood and later that day he came back to see me and said he had told the Commandant that as an officer I could not give my word not to escape. Kurt continued and said he explained to the Commandant that in my physical condition I couldn't get very far. (In my own mind I had to agree, I really couldn't travel very far on foot.) The Commandant agreed with Kurt and gave Kurt permission to take me out of the ward for walks around the compound area. Although my feet hurt a lot when I walked, I looked forward to these walks with Kurt. During these walks around the compound, no one was with us and Kurt gave me information on the progress of the war. The Nazis had forbidden Germans to listen to the British Broadcasting Company (BBC), but many Germans listened anyway. Kurt would bring me up to date on what the BBC had said about the progress of the Allied Forces. At the end, Kurt would always comment that the German military commanders said they had stopped the latest allied advance. Then he would look at me as if to say we both know that isn't so.

This converted-to-a-hospital military compound was on a hill overlooking the town of Arnsberg. One day while Kurt and I were taking a walk around the grounds, the air raid sirens began to wail, sounding the alarm that enemy aircraft were nearby. Kurt did not appear to be alarmed and we stood there watching as six American A-20 light bombers came in at low altitude over the rail yard. To be more specific, five A-20's came over the rail yards and released their bombs on target. The sixth A-20 was completely out of formation and trailed by several hundred yards, but he also dropped his bombs simultaneously with the lead A-20's. The bombs from the out of formation aircraft struck in a residential area. Kurt immediately turned to me and asked why did they bomb the houses. I was very perturbed by the lack of flying discipline displayed by the pilot of the trailing aircraft and I explained to Kurt that the pilot of the last plane must be young and very inexperienced. With that explanation I assumed the incident would be forgotten. A short time later, after I had returned to my ward in the hospital, Kurt and several German officers came to me and asked me if it was a policy of the Americans to bomb civilians. (I guess they had never been told about the activities of the German Luftwaffe or chose to forget.) I was informed that eight civilians had been killed by the plane that bombed the residential area and the townspeople were very upset. It seems that the townspeople had heard that an American pilot was in the hospital and they were demanding that he be brought into town, supposedly to explain what had occurred. How could I explain the deaths, injuries and destruction that result from war? Again I stated that American policy was to strike at military targets and not civilian residential areas (of course I knew that on occasion some of our bombs were dropped rather indiscriminately). My eyes searched the faces of the German officers and I wondered if I would be taken into town. I had heard about Allied airmen who had fallen into the hands of irate civilians, who were victims of bombing raids, and did not live to tell about it. After what seemed like a long time, the ranking officer got up to leave and signaled the others to follow. Kurt explained to me that he would try to calm the townspeople, who evidently had not experienced an attack on their town until now. I was glad to see them leave and had some comfort in the thought that Allied airmen were striking at towns not previously targeted. To me this meant only one thing: the Allies were on the move! I thanked the Lord I didn't have to go face the hostile townspeople and prayed for a quick advance of the Allied Forces.

Several days later, during early evening, the air raid sirens began wailing and all ambulatory patients and civilians who worked at the hospital and their families were herded to the cellars under the buildings. I could hear the droning of aircraft flying overhead. I knew that the British were the only ones who bombed at night, and I also knew, that more than likely, they would be dropping incendiary type bombs in re-payment for the burning of London by the Luftwaffe. Tonight Arnsberg was one of the targets of the British aircraft. Incendiary bombs were dropped over a wide area including the temporary hospital area. Many fires were started by the incendiaries according to reports from the German fire marshals. Again, the Germans, both military and civilians, were asking me why the Americans bombed the hospital and residential areas without discrimination. I carefully tried to explain that Americans did not do any night bombing and that the attacking aircraft had to be British "Tommies". They accepted my explanation, more or less.

In the cellar bomb shelter where we huddled were several young children. The children probably belonged to some of the civilians that worked at the hospital. The children were frightened and confused and I began to pray for their safety. One older man noticed that I was praying and came over to comfort me. His concern for me was unexpected. I pointed my finger at myself and shook my head, then I pointed at the children and he understood my concern. My concern was not without cause for our building had been hit by incendiary bombs and several fires were started. The fires, which were confined to the roof, were extinguished and after about an hour we were allowed to leave the cellar and return upstairs.

A few days later Kurt and I were taking a walk around the grounds when again the air raid sirens began to wail. I could see a lone British fighter bomber diving on a target beyond the next hill. I was unable to see the British fighter pull out from the bomb run. The next day Kurt told me that aircraft had been shot down and the pilot was killed while dive bombing a bridge.

After I had been at Arnsberg for several weeks, Kurt and I were taking a walk around the compound, when he said he had some news for me, but cautioned me not to discuss it with anyone. He said the BBC reported that the Americans had crossed the Rhine River at Ramagen (the bridge at Ramagen was crossed on March 7, 1945). There was no doubt that Kurt knew that Germany was losing the war and it was only a matter of time before the end.

One day Kurt came to me and said that the Commandant was upset that I had not officially been registered as a prisoner of war. He was concerned that the Allies would question why I had not been registered and what had they, the Germans, intended to do with me. So I was officially put on the record as a prisoner of war. Obviously the Commandant knew that the defeat of Germany was near. The next day Kurt indicated that when the American troops reached Arnsberg this would be a combat area, and my safety would be in jeopardy. He said he would package up some provisions for me and would hide me in a safe place until the Americans established control. What he was indicating was that the Germans might shoot me as they retreated. I thanked Kurt for his concern and wondered when the Yanks would reach Arnsberg.

CHAPTER TEN

The Pow Hospital At Hemer, Germany

I didn't get to see the Americans enter Arnsberg, for the next morning I was awakened before daylight and was told I was being transferred to a prisoner of war hospital at Hemer, Germany. A burly German Sergeant, who spoke no English, was assigned as my escort and guard. I never got a chance to say good-bye to Kurt or Elsa. The Sergeant led me a short distance to a truck that was powered by gas generated by a coke burning unit. We climbed into the truck bed and I noted that it was a cold, cloudy day and I didn't expect any Allied planes to be flying due to the unfavorable weather. The driver of the truck proceeded a short distance, then he stopped and began loading 10-gallon milk cans. My guard, the Sergeant, helped load the milk cans and motioned for me to help him. I had loaded milk cans at our farm and I couldn't see why I couldn't handle a few milk cans. I grabbed a milk can by the handles and gave a tug but nothing happened. I didn't have the strength to lift a 10-gallon can full of milk. So I shook my head and backed away from the milk can. The Sergeant again motioned for me to help. I pointed at my 1st Lieutenant's bar and said "Oberlieutenant, nichts worken", and I hoped he was well versed in the Geneva Treaty provisions. He muttered something (presumably not very complimentary) and shook his head in disgust. I wanted him to know I wouldn't work because I was an officer and officers were not required to work, even if they were prisoners of war. I didn't want him to know I was too weak to lift the milk can. The Sergeant finished loading the milk cans and the truck proceeded down the road.

The breeze created in the back of the truck felt quite cold and I was grateful that I had managed to retain possession of my leather flight helmet. At least my head and ears were warm. As we passed through the countryside, even in my unenviable circumstances as a POW, I couldn't help but admire the beautiful valleys and hills of the area. We traveled about 10 kilometers before the truck stopped and the driver informed us that was as far as he was going. The Sergeant inquired as to how far it was to the POW hospital in the town of Hemer. The driver said about 8 kilometers down the road. I noticed that there were civilian laborers constructing tank traps and obstacles along the road. I later learned the workers were slave laborers, mostly prisoners of war and civilians from Russia.

My Sergeant escort was anxious to get started on our way and waved me on. I started at a slow walk with my feet hurting at every step. After proceeding about a hundred yards, I sat down to rest my feet, which felt raw. I quickly surmised that if I had to walk 8 kilometers I probably wouldn't have any feet left by the time we got to the POW hospital. I instantly decided I didn't want to end up with no feet. Nope, I didn't want to go home with no feet. After a short rest, the German Sergeant was ready to go and he indicated that by gesturing in the direction he wanted to travel. I shook my head "no" and pointed at my feet. Once again he gestured insistently that he wanted to get moving on down the road. Again I shook my head and made no effort to get up from my sitting position. With a muttering sound, which I assumed was disapproval or disgust, or both, he reached for his holstered pistol. He pulled his pistol out of the holster and pointed the weapon right at my face! The moment of truth had arrived and my life was in danger once again! I looked at the barrel of the pistol just a few inches from my face and then I looked the Sergeant in the eyes. Once again I pointed at my feet and shook my head "no". The Sergeant continued to point the pistol at my face for what seemed to be a long period of time, but probably it was not more than a minute. By the look on his face I knew he was mentally struggling to decide what his next move would be. I was holding my breath as I wondered what my fate would be! He could shoot me and have the slave laborers bury me and that would be the end. He could report that I had tried to escape and he had to shoot me.

Praise the Lord, the Sergeant was a good soldier and did not want to commit murder. He holstered his pistol and began looking around the countryside, as if somewhere out there was a solution to this unexpected development that was keeping him from delivering his prisoner as ordered. As the Sergeant stood pondering the situation, I also was wondering what happens now. We didn't have to wait long for the Lord's solution to our mutually vexing problem. Over the hill, to our left, there was a one-horse shay approaching us (I firmly believe it was the Lord's timing). As the horse and buggy drew near I could see that an elderly gentleman, dressed in a black suit and wearing a black hat, was driving the buggy. The elderly gentleman was in his late seventies or early eighties and his suit appeared to be as old as the war, which was now in its sixth year. The horse pulling the shay was almost as old as the driver of the shay. The poor horse looked to be so weak it couldn't stand up, not alone pull a buggy. I had seen sway-backed horses back in the USA, but I had never seen a sway-backed horse such as this. The animal's spine dipped at least six inches below the normal position. The Sergeant stopped the old gentleman and his sway-backed horse, said a few words and motioned for me to climb into the shay. I had to hide a smile as I thought of the unusual mode of transportation the Lord had provided at a most critical time. The old man and the sway-backed horse were almost unbelievable. I thanked God for providing transportation and had confidence that the old horse would last long enough to get us eight kilometers down the road.

After about a two hour ride in the one-horse shay, pulled by the faithful old sway-backed horse, we arrived in the small town of Hemer, Germany. The Sergeant made an inquiry of one of the residents and there was a brief exchange, including pointing. We continued a short distance and stopped at a windowless brick building surrounded by an eight-foot high fence topped with several strands of barbed wire. A lone German guard unlocked the gate and I was ushered into the building.

I found myself in a large, windowless room with wooden bunks arranged along each wall. The beds had straw-filled mattresses (and I use the term loosely) on flat boards. The guard, who ushered me in, pointed to a vacant bunk and said "Here", and left the room. I stood there looking around the room trying to absorb everything that was before me. Approximately twenty-five men were in the room, either standing in small groups and conversing, or lying on their bunks. At the moment I was brought into the room, all eyes were turned in my direction. I could see that the men were wearing uniforms of several different Allied Armed Forces. There were American, Belgian, French, Canadian, Australian and British, all captured soldiers. They approached me and asked "When were you captured?". I realized the importance of my answer to their question: If I were recently captured, I would be a current source of news regarding the progress of the war. When I replied I had been captured several weeks ago, there was a noticeable loss of interest in what news I might have. However, their interest was instantly renewed when I told them I had heard the latest news broadcast over BBC Radio, thanks to my friend Kurt back at Arnsberg. They had not heard that the Americans had crossed the Rhine River at

Remagen. Hearing this news created a buzz of excitement in the room and I was pressed for additional information. The fact that the Yanks had crossed the Rhine River and had established a beachhead was truly heartening news. The Rhine River was always considered to be a major obstacle to the Allied advance into Germany. I soon learned that all of the men in this first room were officers and that this installation was considered to be a POW Hospital. One of the men pointed to a vacant bunk covered with a straw-filled mattress and said I could bunk there.

I was given a tour of the remainder of the one story structure and was introduced to over a hundred POW's, many of whom were seriously wounded and were not ambulatory. Medical aid was next to nothing and many of the wounds were infected. As I went from group to group I made certain that everyone heard the encouraging news that the Yanks had crossed the Rhine River. It was during my tour through the hospital that I met Eddie, a young slim built lad from Chicago. Eddie was bedridden with a serious shrapnel wound in his back. I was shocked at the apparent seriousness of the wound and at the lack of medical attention he had received. However, my feelings were uplifted by the totally unexpected cheerful attitude of this young fellow. I made it a point to visit with him at least every morning and afternoon and prayed for physical strength for him.

Many of the occupants of this POW Hospital had recovered from wounds or ailments, and were relatively healthy. Naturally they complained of the lack of food and that was understandable, since all of us were always hungry.

The men were constantly making bets with one another about anything that brought up a difference of opinion, such as what the weather would be tomorrow, what day we would be liberated, who the liberating forces would be, who would win the World Series, etc. The bets were never for money, the stakes always had to do with food, such as "I'll bet you a turkey dinner......". One fellow I remember always started his wager by saying, "I'll bet you five chocolate cream pies.........". Some of the POW's became irritated by the constant references to food, and would move beyond earshot of the always "betting" GI's.

Our daily rations consisted of a small slice of black bread in the morning, a bowl of watery soup at noon, and a bowl of hot water that was mixed with the soup remaining from the noonday ration. It was sufficient to sustain life and no more. Every POW lost weight on the rations provided. The only one who didn't grouse about the food and lack of it was Eddie. I admired his upbeat attitude and during my visits with him I kept telling him it wouldn't be long before we would be liberated by the rapidly advancing American Forces. I enjoyed visiting with Eddie and I believe he raised my spirits as much as I hoped I did his.

Back at the front room of the make-shift POW hospital I met Art, who was a B-17 pilot from Chicago. As Art related it to me, his plane was shot down on his 25th mission, his last before being rotated back to the States. The lead bombardier did not drop the bombs on the first pass over the target, for whatever reason, and the bomber squadron had to make a second orbit over the target. Flying over a heavily defended target one time was hazardous enough, but to orbit the target for a second pass was usually courting disaster. The target was near Cologne, Germany, an area noted for heavy anti-aircraft fire. Disaster did strike Art's B-17. It was disabled by the accurate anti-aircraft fire and the crew had to bail out. One of the flak bursts struck behind and under the pilot's seat and both calves of Art's legs were lacerated by shrapnel. Although the wounds had not healed completely, Art was able to walk, but not without a great deal of pain. Art and I, both being Air Corps pilots, felt a close relationship with each other and spent many hours in conversation.

From the outset I noticed that several of the POW's in the large room spent considerable time scrutinizing their clothing and picking at the seams. I soon learned the reason for this seemingly strange routine. The conditions at this POW hospital were, literally, lousy. All of the beds were infested with lice that quickly infested the clothing of the occupant. Since everyone slept in the one set of clothing they were wearing when captured, the lice remained in the clothing once they found a live body they could feed upon. The lice usually hid in the seams of shirts, especially the seams across the shoulders. The small insects were active enough to irritate the skin and create a narrow, reddish band extending across the shoulders. As disconcerting as the lice were, one learned to put up with their presence. Our only retaliation was to take off our shirts daily and, using a thumb and forefinger, smash all of the lice we could see along the seams. This may have reduced their number but never got rid of them, since there were always more.

The time moved slowly at the POW hospital in Hemer, Germany. One day we were all told we would be permitted to take a hot shower. This announcement was a welcome one, since most of us had not showered or bathed in weeks. Bathing served to cleanse the skin, but afterward we put on our louse infested clothing when we were through. But a shower under any circumstances was welcome.

After I had been in the POW hospital several weeks, all of the ambulatory patients were awakened one morning by German soldiers and ordered to assemble. We were told by one of the German soldiers that we were going to be moved to a location on the other side of the town. There was no transportation provided and all POW's who were considered ambulatory were to walk to the new location. My friend Art, the B-17 pilot, was able to be on his feet but he didn't know how far he could walk, as the wounds in the calves of his legs had not healed completely. Three or four German soldiers armed with rifles were assigned to escort approximately one hundred POW's through town. The first few hundred yards were traversed without incident, but as we neared the town square, we could see a large number of belligerent civilians gathered along the street. As our ragged column of POW's started to pass by the residents of the town, their shouts became increasingly hostile. Without warning they began to throw rocks at us. The German soldiers urged us to hurry, and made half-hearted attempts to keep the enraged civilians away from our marching column. We were all trying to hurry and shield ourselves from the rocks being hurled into our midst. Our rapid pace was beginning to tell on Art and his legs began to falter and he said "Al, I don't know if I can make it". "Don't worry, Art, I'll help you", I said, as I placed my arm around him. With added strength I didn't know I had, I half carried Art along the road. After about a quarter of a mile we were able to get away from the angry citizenry.

Near the end of our forced march, we climbed a hill at the edge of town, where we were ushered into a large building which at one time had been a monastery. The building we entered was one of several that made up a walled-in compound. I was assigned to a room occupied by seven other individuals whom I had not previously met. One of the men came over to me and introduced himself, speaking very good English. He stated that he was a Presbyterian minister and had been held captive for several years. The other six occupants of the room all nodded politely, but did not speak to me. The minister noted that I wore a Catholic medal around my neck and informed me that a Catholic priest would be saying Mass tomorrow morning (Sunday) and showed me the room where the service would be. The next morning I went to Mass at the designated place and I noticed that the priest celebrating the Mass looked familiar, although I couldn't recall why. After church I returned to my room and in a short time a priest entered the room. The priest I saw at Mass was one of my roommates. I soon learned that I had six Catholic priests and a Presbyterian minister for roommates. Well, I thought, if God hears prayers, I should be well protected with the roommates I have.

From the courtyard of the monastery it was possible to look down at the entire town of Hemer. I couldn't help but wonder how Eddie was doing in the POW hospital.

Several hundred yards down the hill towards town there were two large barbed wire encircled compounds that contained about 12,000 slave laborers, mostly Russians. These were the laborers who were forced to repair the damage that Allied air forces created during the day. However, at this stage of the war, very little repair work was even attempted. The slave laborers had been worked day and night and were treated most inhumanely. They were on a starvation diet and lived in conditions of squalor. As we watched the activities in the slave labor compound, we observed bodies of men who died during the night being carried on canvas litters to a burial ground. About a dozen bodies were carried out daily. The bodies of the dead men were so wasted that the weight of the starved corpses hardly made a dent in the canvas litter as they were being carried.

The author just before take-off on a combat mission from an airstrip near Jodoigne, Belgium. (1945)

CHAPTER ELEVEN
Sure Signs That Liberation Was Near

About mid-afternoon, a week after we had moved to the walled-in monastery, we observed a P-51 fly over the compound and drop a bomb which exploded in midair and scattered leaflets all over town. None of the leaflets landed where we could reach them, but we all agreed they must be surrender leaflets. The leaflets were used to offer safe passage to anyone, soldiers or civilians, who carried a leaflet into our lines and surrendered. The delivery of the leaflets also indicated that the town would, in the near future, be under attack from the advancing Allied forces. That same evening while looking across the town toward the surrounding hills, I spotted a large artillery piece mounted on a railroad car. These weapons were known as railroad guns and were of large caliber and capable of firing a shell several miles. While I was watching the railroad gun it began to fire with a loud report. The missile could be heard going through the air and shock waves were visible along its path. This was interesting to me, a pilot, not used to ground warfare. But most interesting of all was to see the railroad gun fire to the left, turn 90 degrees, and fire again, and turn 180 degrees to the right and fire again. It was obvious that we were surrounded on three sides by Allied forces. The news of the railroad gun's action spread among the POW's in the compound and an air of excitement and expectation was everywhere! We all felt that liberation was near. Nothing unusual occurred the next day but our anticipation continued to grow with each passing hour. The following day we heard the sound of aircraft over the town and rushed out to see what was happening. I saw a P-47 with V5 markings - my squadron! The P-47 pilots were over the area looking for designated targets or for targets of opportunity.

Suddenly, an anti aircraft battery began firing at one of the P-47's. The tracers and bursting 40 mm flak came close to one of the Thunderbolts. The pilot realized his vulnerability and hastily changed directions. The flak battery was located on a flak tower, in some trees on the ridge on the other side of town, not far from where the railroad gun had been. The pilot of the P-47, targeted by the flak battery, noticed the location of the flak tower and with eight 50 CAL machine guns blazing the P-47, attacked the flak battery with a vengeance. After the strafing run by the P-47, the flak battery was silent for a time. When the flak battery resumed firing, I observed that the tracers from the battery did not remotely come close to any of the roving P-47's. It appeared, as though, whoever was manning the flak guns was firing away from the P-47's so as not to antagonize them. I chuckled to myself and mused that I wouldn't want to antagonize them either. With the showing of the P-47's over our area, we were certain that the Allied attack was imminent. The next day we were all eagerly watching and listening for signs of the impending attack. About noon a white phosphorus shell exploded in the center of the town square. One of the infantry POW's said "Uh, oh , here it comes!" Within seconds, a great number of artillery shells exploded simultaneously throughout the town. According to an artillery officer friend of mine, we were witnessing a "time on target" barrage. We all ducked away from the open windows and sought shelter within the rock walls of the monastery. No one wanted to be a target for a parting shot by the retreating Germans or a burst of fire by the advancing Yanks. A brisk but short-lived spattering of small arms fire could be heard outside the walls of our compound. The Germans began to withdraw in the face of an overwhelming attack. In just a matter of minutes the small arms fire stopped, except for an occasional round or two. All at once an American GI poked his rifle into the room I was in and slowly looked around! I greeted him warmly and he sat down to take a "breather" as he put it. Our first contact with friendly troops was with a Corporal of the 7th Armored Infantry! Praise the Lord, our liberation as POW's was at hand! The Corporal and I talked for a few minutes before I asked him if he needed to rejoin the chase of the retreating Germans. He said he'd had enough for the day and to follow the retreating Germans into the dense forest would only make him an easy target for snipers, who usually covered a retreat. I offered no comment against such logic, but requested the Corporal to follow me to the arsenal room where the Germans had some small arms and ammunition stored. We managed to open the door to the room and looked over the collection of rifles, submachine guns and pistols. I located a luger pistol and a German submachine gun, known as a "burp gun" because of its "burp, burp" sound when fired. The Corporal cautioned me not to fire the burp gun since it would immediately draw the attention of GI's in the area. It was a point well taken. However, I took the burp gun along, just in case I needed some protection. After several minutes of quiet on the battlefield, I suggested to the Corporal that he and I should go down to the Administration Headquarters and look for some souvenirs (typical Yank behavior). We cautiously poked our heads out the gate leading through the stone wall of the compound when a rifle bullet ricocheted from the wall above our heads. We ducked back inside. The snipers the Corporal had referred to were still a threat. After waiting inside the stone monastery building for several minutes we mutually decided to try to get down to the German Administration Headquarters building. We cautiously left the walled compound and ran for the Headquarters building. No enemy fire came our way and all we could hear was small arms fire in the distance where the Yanks were pursuing the retreating Germans. The run from the monastery to the Headquarters building took more energy than I expected, and in my exhilarated state and weakened condition I had to take a minute to catch my breath. The 7th Armored Infantry Corporal stayed right at my side. We cautiously entered the Administration Headquarters building with our weapons at a ready position. In the main office we encountered a well fed German Major and a big, burly German Sergeant. Neither man offered to make any hostile movement as we approached them. We looked around the room and saw nothing that we thought would be a worthwhile souvenir, and then I saw a safe in the corner of the room. I motioned to the Major to open the safe. He reluctantly complied, but all that was in the safe was money - worthless German marks. I noticed that the German Sergeant was wearing a wrist watch, and I needed one since the Germans who captured me took my watch. I motioned to the Sergeant to give me his watch and he refused, stating that it was "private" and not army issue. I said, "Yeah, that's what I said", referring to when the Germans liberated my wrist watch. I spoke to my Corporal friend, who was closely watching the proceedings and said, "Act like you're going to hit him in the face with the butt of your rifle". The Corporal raised his rifle in the threatening gesture and the German Sergeant quickly gave me his wrist watch. The tide of the battle had changed and now I had liberated a wrist watch.

We left the office and the two Germans and proceeded to the basement of the building. In the basement we found a French POW and a Russian slave laborer. The Russian was reaching for a single cured ham that was hanging from a nail. The Frenchman shoved the starved and weakened Russian from the ham and took the ham from the nail. In the meantime, the Russian had found a hatchet lying nearby and had raised it above his head, intending to bury it in the back of the Frenchman's skull. I quickly reached from behind the Russian and took the hatchet from his upraised arm. With my burp gun submachine gun I motioned for the Frenchman to give the ham to the emaciated Russian. I explained to the Corporal that the French POW's had American Red Cross food parcels that supplemented the Prison Hospital rations and they had more to eat than the rest of us. They guarded their Red Cross parcels closely and never shared the food with any of us - the law of survival I guess you'd call it. Anyway, I chased the Frenchman out of the building and the Russian thanked me for the ham. The Frenchman probably never realized how close he had come to getting a severe headache from the hatchet wielding Russian. Next the Corporal and I went to the guardhouse at the entrance to the slave labor compound. No one was there but a young Belgian girl. She explained that she had been forced to work for the Germans for several years and she appeared at a loss as to what to do next. The young girl, I noticed was aged beyond her years and had a deep, sad look in her eyes. She had undoubtedly endured untold hardships while in German hands. In the guard house we found a loaf of black bread and some bologna from which we made a sandwich. The Corporal didn't relish his sandwich, but any kind of food tasted good to me, however, I was cautious not to eat too much after being on starvation rations for several months. After we finished our sandwich, I decided to return to my "quarters" in the monastery on the hill.

Upon entering the monastery I was met by my Presbyterian minister roommate. He seemed anxious to talk with me. He said that the Russian slave laborers were threatening to break out of the compound. A small group of

American soldiers remained behind the advancing troops and were anxious to keep the Russian slave laborers from entering the town. The Russians undoubtedly harbored deep feelings of hatred toward Germans and would not hesitate to pillage the town and kill the civilians that remained. Two American tanks were parked in the entrances to the compound to contain the twelve thousand slave laborers. The situation was becoming more volatile by the minute.

My friend, the Presbyterian minister, who was fluent in the Russian language, had volunteered to speak to the Russian slave laborers to try to calm them. He wanted an American Officer POW to accompany him. I asked, "Why do you need me to go with you?" He replied, "They won't listen to me, but if you, an American Officer POW, accompany me, they will listen." I analyzed the situation quickly and asked the minister "What are you going to tell them?" He replied that he would tell them to be patient and keep calm, and that a Russian Mission Force was on the way. The Mission would arrive within a few hours and would start their repatriation as soon as possible. I kind of smiled to myself and said "Why don't you let me tell them?" "They wouldn't understand you", he said. "I'll tell them in Russian", I replied. He looked surprised and then queried, "Do you speak Russian?" I explained that my mother had emigrated from Russia, and I learned Russian as a child since it was spoken in the family. We proceeded down to the first of two compounds, where approximately seven thousand Russian slave laborers had gathered in the fenced area. We stood on a small platform that was about three feet high. As the two of us stood there, the Russians were mildly curious and quite noisy and boisterous. I looked over this large group of old men, young men, and boys and then in a moderately loud voice I said in Russian: "Listen to me!" Surprisingly, a hush fell over the large group and I continued to speak in Russian. I paused and asked if they understood me. They said, "Yes, yes, we understand you." I continued to speak for just a few moments and encouraged them to "hang on", that help was coming soon and they would be going home. As I finished speaking one gaunt-faced man looked up at me and, speaking in Russian, said, "Some of us will make it and some of us will not". Sadly, I nodded my head, for I needed no explanation; I had seen the daily passage of the canvas litters bearing the bodies of men who had not survived the night.

A young Russian boy came out of the crowd and asked me if I thought the liberated German Luger pistol I had tucked under my belt was a good souvenir. I nodded my head in answer. He disappeared and quickly returned and handed me a leather holster with a Luger pistol in it. He said they had taken it from a German Sergeant and that I could have it. As I thanked him for the Luger, the Presbyterian minister reminded me that we had another group of about five thousand slave laborers who needed to hear about the Russian Mission Force.

As I spoke to the second group of Russians I received the same rapt attention that I received from the first group. My heart went out to these mistreated individuals who had been caught up in a world at war, and had borne such hardships and indignities. The main question I was asked by several individual Russians was "Where did you learn to speak Russian?" I explained that my mother was born in Russia and I learned from her. After the Presbyterian minister and I departed from the compound I asked him, "How did I do, do you think they understood?" Unexpectedly he said that I had done very well, but most of all it was my sympathetic tone of voice that was most effective. He explained that these men had not heard a sympathetic word in years. It was discouraging and saddening to witness the cruelty man heaps upon fellow man. At this time I was not even aware of the existence of the death camps where the German military and police had put to death millions of Jewish men, women and children.

My minister friend and I returned to the monastery where an American Major from SHAEF (Supreme Headquarters Allied Expeditionary Forces) based in Paris, was speaking to a group of Americans who had been POW's. Another fighter pilot, who had been shot down only a few days prior, and I listened as the Major instructed us to stay where we were and we would be evacuated later in the day; as he spoke it was a little after 1300 hours (one o'clock). My fighter pilot companion and I concurred that the Major was Army and we were Air Corps, and we didn't necessarily have to follow his orders. We both noticed the creases in his shirt and trousers, which indicated that he probably fought the war sitting on his butt in an office. I informed the Major of the wounded in the POW hospital in the center of the town, as I was concerned about the wounded, especially Eddie. As he turned to leave, we informed him that we would wait till 15:00 hours (3:00 p.m.) and if he had not returned we would leave on our own. The Major must have been a bit upset to have two First Lieutenants tell him what they were going to do.

By three o'clock neither the SHAEF Major nor any of his organization were to be found. So, true to our word, my fighter pilot companion and I liberated a Duesenberg automobile and proceeded to leave the town of Hemer. My companion (I couldn't recall his name) had flown missions in the area only a few days before and was familiar with the area. He indicated that there was a captured German airfield a few miles down the road where we could probably catch a ride back to France. As we traveled up the hill out of Hemer we came to a wide open field that was filled with row after row of artillery pieces, the smaller guns up front and the larger, longer range guns toward the rear. It was no surprise that the Germans retreated so rapidly when confronted by such a tremendous array of military fire power. To me, a fighter pilot, the array of artillery was certainly impressive. My fighter pilot colleague knew where he was going and in a few minutes we arrived at the captured German airfield. The airfield had been occupied by American forces for several days. The facilities had sleeping accommodations, hot showers and a mess hall set up for field grade officers (rank of Major and above). I entered the mess hall by myself since my fighter pilot friend chose not to follow me. I guess he wasn't as hungry as I was since he had only been a POW for less than a week. The Majors and Colonels eating in the mess hall gave me a quizzical look as I entered wearing my POW attire, consisting of a French beret, an Australian battle jacket, OD trousers and black boots. In addition, I had a pair of German binoculars slung over my neck and two German Lugers hanging from my belt. The only insignia I had left was a first lieutenant's bar on my shirt collar. The Germans, at the hospital in Arnsburg, had taken my Air Corps insignia and pilots wings for souvenirs while I was asleep. I'm not sure what the Field Grade Officers thought of me entering and eating in their mess. However, no one challenged me, in fact, no one spoke to me. Maybe they thought I was a member of the French Forces of Resistance. Despite the questioning glances in my direction I enjoyed my best meal in months. I thanked the Lord for my food and for my safe return to the American Armed Forces.

Next came a hot shower and a good scrubbing to get rid of any lice and lice eggs that were liberated with me. My lice infected clothing was discarded and I was given new shoes, shorts, tee shirt, shirt and trousers. By nightfall truckloads of liberated POW's were arriving from the monastery and some from the POW hospital in Hemer. Several of them wondered how I had arrived at the captured German Airfield before they did, but their curiosity didn't last for long when I told them hot showers, clean clothes and good food was available. I was informed that the more seriously wounded POW's, including Eddie, were evacuated by American medics.

In the evening, after supper, we were given the opportunity to write home (V-mail) to our loved ones and inform them that we were still among the living. In most instances the International Red Cross had no record of Allied Armed Forces personnel taken prisoner in the latter stages of the war. Having written to my parents and to my fiancee, LaVon, I settled down in the luxury of a clean bed, without lice, to enjoy the full realization that I was liberated and would soon be going to my fighter squadron, I thought. It felt as though a heavy burden had been lifted from my shoulders. Due to the excitement of the day's events - April 14, 1945 - and due to the caffeine in the coffee, which I was not accustomed to drinking, the night seemed long and falling asleep seemed impossible.

Morning arrived after a few hours sleep, breakfast was served early, and everyone was alerted to be prepared to "fall out" and be ready to be air lifted back to France. Shortly the order came and we lined up in a single, long line on the airfield. The Major from SHAEF inspected the line of men. Some of the enlisted POW's had liberated numerous wrist watches so that both arms had wrist watches from the wrist to the elbow. Others had liberated shotguns and handguns. All of these souvenirs were liberated after my friend and I had left the town of Hemer at three o'clock the previous afternoon. It was evident from the large number of souvenirs carried by each enlisted former POW, that the liberated GI's had been busy collecting souvenirs. After walking up and down the line of men the Major stopped in front of me and said, "It looks like you are the ranking officer of this group". I made no comment since we would be divided into small groups and loaded into C-47 transports for our flight to France. No officer need be in charge of the liberated men since the C-47 air crew would be in charge. The Major eyed my two Luger pistols and finally said, "You can't take those back with you". For a second I was intimidated by this statement and asked, "How much are they worth to you?" I knew from experience that a 9mm Luger was one of the prized souvenirs of the war. The Major replied, "I'll give you a thousand francs". A thousand francs was a piddling amount and I replied, "Major, I'll throw these into the harbor first before I give them up. Furthermore, let me caution you, these men have all been toughened by combat and have not been under discipline for quite a while. If you try to take any of their souvenirs, I can't guarantee your safety." After my statement, the Major lost interest in confiscating anyone's souvenirs. I figured he wanted some souvenirs for himself, but wasn't willing to take the risk of antagonizing any of the liberated GIs who intended to keep all the souvenirs they had liberated.

CHAPTER TWELVE
Homeward Bound

We boarded the C-47 transport planes in groups of about twenty and took off for France - Goodbye Germany.

To me, who was accustomed to the speed of a P-47, the C-47 transport plane seemed to be very slowly flying over the countryside; but, after less than two hours we landed in France and were transported in Army trucks to a tent city called Camp Lucky Strike. Camp Lucky Strike was established to process newly arrived army units going to the front, and to process prisoners of war that were anticipated to be returning in increasing numbers. Our group of former POW's was among the first to be processed. Since Stalag VI A was only a few kilometers on the other side of the Rhine River, we were among the first to be liberated by the advancing Allied Forces. Other POW camps were located deep within Germany and their liberation came days and even weeks later.

At Camp Lucky Strike we were being treated with overwhelming kindness. Tragically for one young lad, who was afforded all of the Red Cross donuts he could eat, for he ate too many for his starved body, and his urge to quell his hunger proved fatal. It seemed that no one was sure just how to feed POW's in order to bring us back to a nutritional norm. Anyway, the supply of donuts was limited after the tragic incident, but Praise the Lord, we had more to eat than a slice of black bread and a bowl of watery soup.

Our processing, including physical examinations and the usual military paper work, proceeded rather rapidly. In less than a week we were given orders to proceed to the French port city of Le Havre, where we would board ship for the journey home. Since the war was nearly over, I presumed there was no point in returning me to my squadron. Fifteen men who were returning to Colorado and Wyoming were assigned to my group. I was the only officer in the group and was designated to be commander of Group E436-8. My duties were to see that all of the men placed in my charge arrived at the U.S. Port Reception Center. This assignment was not difficult: once all the men were on board ship there would be no way for anyone to wander away. One incident did occur, as I recall. On the day we were to proceed to Le Havre, all of us went through a final medical check. One of the young men in my group came down with a slight fever, and the nurse in charge decided that he should remain in Camp Lucky Strike until his fever subsided. I was at his bedside, in the large tent being used as a ward, when the nurse gave him the news that he couldn't go with the group to board ship at Le Havre. What he was hearing was that he couldn't go home because he had a slight fever. He looked at me in a pleading manner as though I had the ability to change the situation. The nurse's tone of voice came across as more of a suggestion than a tone of finality. I spoke directly to the nurse and said, "He doesn't look very sick and he's been fine up to now". "Well, he does have a slight fever", she replied. Then came my next question, "Will we have Doctors aboard our ship?" "Yes", she replied, "since your ship will be picking up wounded at Southampton, England before sailing for New York." I seized the moment and said, "Good, let him go with us. I'll look after him and see that he gets medical attention." The nurse agreed and the young man quickly dressed, picked up his duffel bag, and we proceeded to the designated location where we were to be loaded on trucks to go to the seaport at Le Havre. As we walked together toward the waiting trucks, the young man thanked me profusely for not leaving him behind. The remaining fourteen members of my group were already assembled and waiting to load up. I called off each name on my list to make certain all were present. Everyone responded and we boarded the army trucks for the next part of our journey home. After several hours of riding in the trucks we arrived at the wharf at Le Havre, and without further ado we boarded an ocean liner and found our assigned quarters for the voyage home.

The ship was a luxury liner converted to a troop transport. Converted means it would carry five or six times more passengers than it did in peace time. Quarters were cramped but complaints were few. My quarters, designated for officers, were so crowded that I could touch six other bunks without getting up from my bunk, yet I knew that my group of enlisted men were even more crowded. Our ship's Captain waited until nightfall before proceeding across the channel to Southampton, England, where we took aboard a number of wounded American servicemen who were well enough to travel. The reason given for waiting for nightfall was that the German U-boats were still active in the English Channel and the chances of being torpedoed were much less at night.

We sailed from Southampton in a small convoy of relatively fast ships escorted by several Destroyers. There was a slight feeling of uneasiness due to the presence of a threat from German U-boats. Despite the lingering U-boat threat, being aboard the converted luxury liner sailing for home was pleasant from the standpoint that the war was behind us. The shipboard Doctor said that the young GI who had a fever at Camp Lucky Strike was doing well. The Doctor gave me some iron mineral supplement pills to help overcome the anemia from which most POW's suffered. In addition he suggested that we should walk around the deck of the ship as often as we could. Consequently, a great deal of my time was spent walking the promenade deck of the ship. I enjoyed the walking even though my frost-bitten feet blistered easily and my sea legs were wobbly at times.

With my weight at 130 pounds, I realized I had lost 35 pounds in a few short months. However, the feeding program aboard the converted luxury liner was certainly designed to put on a few pounds during our voyage to the United States. Breakfast came first with fresh eggs, instead of the powdered variety that was standard; bacon, ham, pancakes, orange juice and milk, with seconds available upon request. At mid-morning a snack was scheduled with milk, rolls and cookies. Lunch consisted of delicious sandwiches with milk and ice cream served for desert. Dinner, or supper, as we called it, was served early in the evening and was the most looked-forward to meal of the day. The main item for the evening meal was beef and pork with all the trimmings. The favorite was pork chops and a second serving was always requested. In fact, after the first couple of days we usually asked our waiter (oh, yes, we had waiters serving our meals - what luxury for former POW's) to bring a double helping of pork chops at the start of the meal in order to save him an extra trip for seconds. A double order of desert was also requested. The waiters informed us that they were part of the permanent crew aboard the liner. Since supper was served early in the evening, a late evening snack of cake, cookies and milk was available about 2100 hours (9:00 p.m.) for those who were still hungry, and many were. Some of the members of my group had requested duty in the ship's bakery where the baking for the next day's meal was done at night.

Shortly after our departure from England, an announcement was made that all weapons that were brought on board as souvenirs were to be turned in for safe keeping during the voyage home. A dubious statement, assuring the return of the souvenirs once we reached the United States, was made as an afterthought. I assumed that my group of former POW's had collected their share of souvenir weapons after being liberated. The order (or request, as I viewed it), to turn in souvenir weapons for safe keeping, had some merit from a safety standpoint. However, I recognized it was more of a scheme to provide souvenirs for officers in charge who had never been close to the combat zone and had no souvenir weapons, or for those who had souvenirs and wanted more. I gathered my group together and told them I didn't want to see any of their souvenir weapons, and if I didn't see any weapons I would report that my group had no weapons to turn in. In addition, I advised that, if they saw someone with a souvenir weapon, they should tell him to place it in the bottom of his duffel bag and leave it there until he arrived home. A good relationship, with my group of returning POW's, was assured after they had heard how I would handle the "request" for turning in all souvenir weapons for safe keeping.

Since I had proven to my group that I would look after their interests, the men who were pulling duty in the ship's bakery wanted to do something for me. They invited me down to the bakery every midnight where they had some "extra" pies to share with me. The voyage to the States was featured by one meal after another including pie at midnight, and best of all, each day's travel brought us closer to home. I walked the promenade deck as much as possible and the exercise not only built up my stamina, but also increased my appetite for the bonanza of food that was available. The voyage across the Atlantic Ocean lasted eleven days, and toward the end of the voyage our appetites had tapered off considerably and second helping requests were limited to special entrees or deserts. Our ship arrived in New York Harbor during the night, and we did not have an opportunity to see the Statue of Liberty as we neared the

Port of New York. We awakened early in the morning and discovered that our ship was in the harbor and was preparing to dock. We were instructed to get ready to disembark. I made sure that all of my group had heard the order, and were ready to leave the ship. A small group of dock workers and several Red Cross members greeted us as we made our way down the gang plank. We proceeded directly to waiting busses that were to take us to Camp Kilmer, New Jersey. Camp Kilmer was point of departure for many of us when we originally left for overseas duty. We did not have to go through any customs inspections, which was understandable as such a procedure would have been an unnecessary waste of time.

At Camp Kilmer a minimum of processing was necessary, and most of our time was spent obtaining a few items of clothing and some ETO and combat ribbons to wear on our uniforms. I'm certain that quite a few unauthorized ribbons were being worn since no authorization was required for the purchase of ribbons. However, it's understandable that returning POW's wanted to have a "respectable" number of ribbons when they reached home.

After a couple of days, processing was over, and we were transported to a nearby railroad station where we boarded a train heading west to Chicago. Food aboard the train was a far cry from the feast we had aboard ship; however, complaints were minimal as we were heading home. We arrived in Chicago on May 8, 1945, and everywhere news boys were shouting that the war was over in Europe! It was VE Day! Twenty-four days after being liberated from a German POW camp the war in Europe was over! As our train proceeded slowly through Chicago, we passed by buildings where hundreds of workers, who were lined up at the windows, were waving at our troop train and everyone aboard the train was waving back. According to some railroad personnel, a public announcement of the arrival of our troop train had been made earlier, which accounted for the large number of people who greeted our train as we passed through Chicago.

The next stop was Denver, which was the destination of my entire group and, according to orders, my responsibility for the group ended. Upon arrival at the train depot I took a cab to Lowry Field where I received a partial payment so I could purchase items of clothing to complete my uniform. I managed to find the bare essentials in my size. From Lowry Field I took a cab to the bus station where I boarded a bus for Erie, Colorado, which was about four miles from our farm. I was hoping I could find someone in Erie who would have enough gasoline (gasoline was rationed) and be willing to give me a ride home. I got off the bus in Erie, where I had graduated from high school. There were no bands playing, no welcoming parade, no red carpet treatment. Perhaps no one told them I was coming home. Oh well, it was no big deal. I found a telephone in the drug store and called my friend Dewitt. He was home and said he would come and pick me up. Dewitt was a former schoolmate who had a medical discharge from the Army. We greeted each other briefly and talked a bit as we drove the four miles to our farm. The familiar countryside looked good to me. It was about mid-afternoon when we arrived at our farm. As we drove into the farmyard my mother heard our car and came out of the house. I got out of the car and she threw her arms around me, hugging me as only mothers can. Her face and actions expressed the joy of seeing, alive again, her youngest son who had been reported as missing in action. I thanked Dewitt for driving me out to our farm and he left after we agreed to see each other soon. My mother released me from her arms and said I should go and see my father, who was working in the field and didn't know I had arrived. I walked out to where my father was working in the field and, upon reaching him, we hugged each other. Then my father dropped to his knees in thanksgiving to God for my safe return from war. After talking a short time, we both walked back to the house where my mother, my father and I rejoiced that I was alive and back home again. Individually and collectively we thanked God for my safe return. I excused myself for a moment to make a call to LaVon, my fiancee, who was ever so faithful in writing letters with news from home and always closing with an expression of love. The morale boosting effect of letters from home to loved ones in the armed forces can never be overestimated.

Early in the evening I drove up to the Brown residence where LaVon was living with her parents. My arrival was definitely expected and as I got out of the 1933 Ford, I was met with loving arms. It was like a dream come true as I held my lovely young sweetheart in my arms. Reluctantly we broke our embrace long enough for me to greet LaVon's mother and father who had also come out of the house to greet me. LaVon and I were married three weeks after I had arrived home. My wartime sweetheart has been a loving wife and wonderful mother for our children, three boys and a daughter, for over fifty years.

I continue to thank God for the blessings of surviving the most destructive war ever experienced on the earth. A war that claimed the lives of a multitude, including close and dear friends and comrades in arms.

In the days and weeks following my return home I met many relatives and friends who remarked, "We're glad you're back, you sure were lucky". To this day, fifty years later, as I recall my military service in WW II, I know in my heart, without a doubt, it ain't all luck. Thank you, Lord.

Back on the farm after return from the war in Europe.

To order additional copies of **By the Grace of God,** complete the information below.

Ship to: (please print)

Name ______________________________

Address ______________________________

City, State, Zip ______________________________

Phone ______________________________

_____ copies of ***By the Grace...*** @ $7.95 each $ _______

Postage and handling @ $2.00 plus

$1.00 for each additional book $ _______

CO residents add 3.8% sales tax $ _______

Total amount enclosed $ _______

Enclose check or money order payable to ***Al Zlaten***

Send to:
Al Zlaten
1673 Brown Ct
Longmont, CO 80503